GLIMPSES OF GRACE

BY

HARIPRIYA RENGARAJAN

&

RAVI VALLURI

HOLISTIC Publishing

Published by “The Great Indian Book Tour”
Imprint : **Holistic Publishing**
www.tgibt.com
106/91, Ashok marg, Vijay path
Mansarover, Jaipur, Rajasthan-302020
Phone : +91-72400-68114
email : prashant@tgibt.com

Title : **Glimpses of Grace**

Author : **Haripriya Rengarajan/ Ravi Valluri**

Edited by: **Lakshmi Valluri**

First published in 2026
First Edition 2026
Printed in India
Printer : Repro Printers
ISBN : 978-81-69049-19-1

Price :299

Tera Main, Main Tera

Dedicated to millions of followers

of

Gurudev Sri Sri Ravi Shankar

on the auspicious occasion

of

His 70th birthday, 13 May, 2026

A Note to the Reader

Vedic wisdom reminds us that seekers approach truth according to their *adhikāra* – their inner preparedness, temperament, and stage of unfolding. In that spirit, this book speaks through two distinct voices. The narratives that follow differ in cadence, expression, and movement of thought, not as divergences of intent, but as natural expressions of *adhikāra-bheda.*

Each author walks an independent inner path, shaped by unique experiences, questions, and moments of grace, yet both journeys are oriented toward an ineffable Presence. These writings do not seek uniformity of style or convergence of interpretation. They are offerings—complete in themselves—arising from different standpoints of the heart and mind.

The authors invite the reader to receive each of their voices without comparison, to dwell with each account as a standalone journey, and to recognize that Truth does not reveal itself through a single lens. As rivers differ in course yet meet the same ocean, these narratives flow independently, guided by their Gurus, toward that which words can only gesture to.

PROLOGUE

When the disciple is ready, the Guru arrives, they say… and HE does arrive, at the most opportune of times… Some experiences with the Master would remain unfathomable, inexpressible. The most esoteric of knowledge, the most sublime of Wisdom can never ever be understood through words, but only through one's own experience of things, through the profoundest of silence, by just being with the Being.

Yet this endeavor is to provide some experiences of devotees with Gurudev Sri Sri Ravi Shankar, in humble submission to Him…

Om Saha Navavatu Saha Nau Bhunaktu

Saha Viryam Karavavahai

Tejasvinavadhitamastu Ma Vidhvisavahai

Om Shantih Shantih Shantih

Where Grace Speaks Differently

Grace does not arrive with uniformity.
It meets each seeker where the heart is open,
where the inner readiness quietly waits.

What follows is not a continuation,
nor a contrast,
but another manner of listening.

The Higher Presence is the same.
Only the window changes.

INDEX

Chapter 1

Meeting the Master

- Haripriya Rengarajan

Some journeys can be narrated, while others are mystical, transcending the limitations of the human mind. Such has been my journey with my Master. My first notion of him came through a video of the Art of Living Foundation—a fleeting glimpse of the phenomenon that is Gurudev. The sight of millions following him left an indelible impression on my mind. But it was the first up-close encounter that truly altered the course of my life.

I remember standing amidst a sea of people, all yearning for his blessings. As I observed the fervor surrounding him, a question arose within me—why wouldn't they give him some space? Why were they pushing past each other just to get a little closer? While these thoughts lingered, I suddenly found myself caught in his gaze. A pair of eyes, luminous and knowing, met mine from afar, accompanied by a gentle smile. I was unprepared for the moment. Caught off guard, my hands instinctively came together in reverence. That gaze, in a way I did not yet comprehend, was the calling of a lifetime.

At that time, I stood at the crossroads of my long corporate career. The next few months at work felt like a continuous beckoning towards the Art of Living Foundation. During lunch breaks and fleeting moments of respite from my demanding schedule, I would find solace in reading Gurudev's wisdom or watching his videos, which seemed to offer answers to dilemmas I had been grappling with. What I had thought would be a difficult transition—leaving behind my corporate identity—happened effortlessly. I envisioned speaking to him in close quarters, yet I had no idea how that would unfold. Many questions remained unanswered.

After enduring a period of profound inner turmoil and countless moments of self-doubt, there came a beckoning—an opportunity with the Foundation. Initially, I had anticipated a seamless transition into a leadership role, given the senior position I had held at work. But life had a different unfolding. Through a series of trials, I found myself stripped of the identity I once held dear. The titles and roles that had defined me seemed distant; the confidence and conviction that once flowed effortlessly felt obscured. Even my health became something I had to consciously preserve.

Yet, this opportunity arrived like a breath of fresh air—a quiet revival amidst uncertainty. In that sacred space, I experienced a deep sense of peace in the Master's presence, especially through the daily meditations. There was a subtle yet undeniable connection. I found myself waiting for a glimpse of him—not out of longing alone, but out of gratitude for the stillness his presence evoked within me.

Meditation became my sanctuary. At home, however, this inward turning was sometimes met with resistance. The simple act of sitting in silence stirred concern that I might withdraw from the responsibilities of a householder's life. Yet what I truly longed for was integration—a life where contemplation and action could coexist in harmony, where work and meditation nourished one another. Each time I turned within, the mind settled into a quiet clarity, strengthening not escape, but engagement with life.

From that point onward, my journey unfolded through diverse initiatives and roles. It was not always smooth; transformation rarely is. Life led me beyond the Foundation's walls into work as an educationist, author, researcher, and more. Through every transition, one constant remained—my deep reverence for Gurudev.

Over time, I have come to understand that his guidance was never about following a personality, but about being led inward—toward one's own truth. He does not gather seekers around himself; he gently turns them toward their inner selves. What deepened was not dependence, but clarity.

Even now, as I reflect on this journey, my heart fills with quiet gratitude—not with longing, but with recognition of the grace that has shaped my unfolding. His presence is not something to cling to; it is a light that illumines the path within, leaving behind an inner smile that lingers in the deepest corners of my being.

Reflection & Exercises:

➢ As a reader, can you recall a moment in your life when you felt drawn to a higher purpose?

➢ What was your first impression of someone who inspired you deeply?

Personal Journal Page: Note your personal experiences of initial inspiration or guidance from any source.

Chapter 2

The Master's Aura

The Master's Aura—A Presence Beyond Words

There are presences in this world that defy articulation—forces that transcend words, actions, and even conscious comprehension. Some individuals walk into a space, and without uttering a single word, shift the very air around them, infusing it with peace, clarity, and an inexplicable joy. Gurudev Sri Sri Ravishankar is one such presence—a luminous field of love and wisdom where burdens dissolve, questions vanish, and the heart finds itself at home.

"People may forget what you say or do, but they always remember how you make them feel," says a famous adage. Yet what happens when someone's presence makes you feel whole, accepted, and deeply cherished—not for what you should become, but for what you already are? Such is the alchemy of Gurudev's presence. It is an invitation to love oneself, to pause and listen—not merely to the world, but to the whispers of one's own soul. In his aura, self-doubt dissolves, masks fall away, and a profound gratitude arises—not just toward him, but toward life itself.

Words are subject to interpretation, colored by the filters of one's own mind. But presence—true, enlightened presence—is infallible. It speaks in a language beyond thought, beyond the grasp of intellect. A dozen meticulously prepared questions and planned conversations disintegrate in an instant upon seeing him, as though the very act of being in his presence renders them obsolete. What remains is silence—a silence not empty, but full; not passive, but potent. It is in this silence that people find answers they never knew they were seeking.

The Power of Silence: When Questions Disappear

Many individuals have shared how, upon meeting Gurudev, their long-standing doubts and struggles simply vanished. They approached him, ready to articulate their deepest concerns, only to find that the very need to ask dissolved in his presence.

A young seeker once arrived at an advanced meditation course determined to ask Gurudev a fundamental question about the meaning of life. After waiting hours for an opportunity, he finally stood before him, only to realize that the question had lost all relevance. Instead, he was filled with a sense of deep peace, as if the answer had been known all along but only now uncovered.

Another devotee, burdened with years of emotional turmoil, had prepared a long list of philosophical and personal questions. Yet, upon making eye contact with Gurudev, she broke down into uncontrollable tears—not from sadness, but from an overwhelming sense of release. She later shared, "I had spent years searching for answers outside, but in that moment, I realized everything I needed was already within."

Healing Beyond Words: Shedding Deep-Rooted Stress And Trauma Beyond Intellectual Clarity

Gurudev's presence has been a source of profound healing for countless individuals. People who have endured grief, depression, and deep emotional wounds have found inexplicable relief simply by being in his aura.

A woman who had carried the pain of losing her child for over a decade recalled how, in a single *satsang* with Gurudev, she felt as though a weight had been lifted from her heart. "For years, I could not even speak of my loss without breaking down. That evening, as I sat in his presence, I cried like never before—but when the tears stopped, so did my suffering. I felt a peace I had not known in years."

Stories of physical healing also abound. A devotee once came to a meditation retreat struggling with severe migraines that no treatment had been able to cure. After sitting in silence with Gurudev for just a few minutes, she felt an immense wave of relaxation, and from that day forward, the migraines never returned.

Such instances are not anomalies. Many have shared how, even without speaking a word or receiving direct guidance, they have experienced transformations that defy logic. Tears flow effortlessly, lifetimes of burdens dissipate, and a newfound lightness emerges—proof that true healing is not just of the body, but of the soul.

Once during a program there was a woman who, unfiltered and unguarded, confessed every flaw she perceived in herself. "I must be a *rakshasi*," she declared boldly, unafraid of judgment. That moment was not one of despair, but of profound transformation. The next day, her eyes brimming with emotion, she said, "*Ye hi ek hain jo sabko krithagya karke jaate hain*"—he brings forth gratitude in people, not just toward him, but toward life itself. Yet, unlike those who enter and exit one's life, he does not come to leave; he comes to stay, an unseen yet ever-felt presence in the lives of those he touches.

His presence has a way of orchestrating synchronicities beyond rational explanation. There is a well-known story—one he narrates himself, laced with humor and wonder—about a tea bag. In South Africa, on the last day of a visit to Durban, he did something unusual. He walked into a room where his teachers were staying, looked around, and without a word, picked up a tea bag from a table and left. The teachers in the room, startled and puzzled, observed this in silence. Why would Gurudev, who doesn't even drink tea, take a tea bag and walk away?

Later, at the Johannesburg airport, an elderly gentleman approached him with tears in his eyes. "Guruji, did you receive the tea bag I sent for you?"

It turned out that the man had bought that particular tea bag with immense love and had entrusted it to one of the teachers to give to Gurudev. But in the flurry of events, it had been forgotten. And yet, as if moved by an invisible force, Gurudev had found his way to it. "See," he chuckled, "I stole the tea bag!" But behind the laughter lay a truth—an unseen current of connection, where love is received beyond the bounds of space and time.

This is the essence of the enlightened — where presence is the teaching, where silence is the answer, where love is not a sentiment, but a state of being. Gurudev does not merely come and go; he remains, in the quiet spaces of the heart, in the gentle echoes of transformation, and in the silent yet profound shifts that make life infinitely more beautiful.

Transformation in an Instant: Lives Shifted in His Presence

Many individuals have entered Gurudev's gatherings as skeptics, only to leave profoundly transformed. Without any conversation, without any explicit guidance, they experienced a shift in perspective, breaking free from doubts, destructive habits, or limited ways of thinking.

One young man, lost in life and trapped in negative habits, reluctantly attended a *satsang* at the insistence of a friend. Sitting at the back, arms crossed, he observed the gathering with disinterest. However, the moment Gurudev walked in, something shifted within him. A wave of inexplicable emotion swept over him, melting his resistance. By the end of the evening, he felt a renewed sense of purpose. That night, he made a life-altering decision—to quit his self-destructive habits and dedicate himself to a path of service and self-improvement.

Similarly, a high-profile corporate leader, long consumed by stress and an unending pursuit of success, found himself sitting in one of Gurudev's meditation retreats. He had no expectations, but as he sat in silence, he felt something shift. He later shared, "For the first time in years, I felt free. I understood what true success meant—not just achieving goals, but being at peace within." He soon changed his career path, aligning his work with a deeper sense of purpose.

Reflection & Exercises:

➢ Have you ever experienced the aura of a person or a place?

Personal Journal Page: Note how you felt when someone made you feel cherished or understood.

Chapter 3

Experiencing the Master's Benediction

Art of Living faculty member, volunteer, and a railwayman Ravi Valluri, like millions of other devotees, has experienced Glimpses of Grace of the spiritual master. He shares those precious moments of benediction received during his never-ending journey with the Art of Living Foundation.

In Rugged Rajasthan

On the appointed day, Ravi and his family hopped on to a meter–gauge train to Bikaner, for him to take up his new posting in the railways.

Tragically for his family, Ravi was again in an inebriated state, creating a nuisance at the Sarai Rohilla station from where they boarded.

Bikaner is in the north-western part of Rajasthan which has extreme climes. During summers the weather is scorching and sapping, though evenings are generally tolerable. As the sun sinks in the sands of the deserts and shadows lengthen, nights turn very cold touching zero and sub-zero temperatures, especially during winters.

Meanwhile it was a crisp and chilly morning on December 13, 2001, in Delhi, when a blood thirsty cell of five armed men attacked the Parliament of India by breaching the security cordon at Gate 12. The five men killed seven security personnel before being eliminated by the Indian security forces.

On December 20, despite frantic calls from the United States, Russia, and the United Nations to exercise restraint, India mobilized and deployed its troops to Kashmir, Punjab, and Rajasthan in what became India's largest military mobilization since the 1971 conflict. India code-named this massive mobilization as Operation *Parakram.*

In those trying conditions, despite being under the influence of alcohol, he braced himself for the challenge and marshalled his troops consisting of all the railway control staff, and other operating staff at stations and terminals who were in turn ably supported by other departments of railways to handle military specials.

Today, he recalls those wintry weekends in Bikaner, when he hit the bottle after performing a part of his official duties where he oversaw passenger and freight operations and military movement.

It was a strange fixation with the drink. He vomited only to drink more. One could call it drinking bulimia. As darkness spread across the deserts of Rajasthan and shadows lengthened in the railway bungalow, he was battling to handle the second bottle of gin.

As a routine, it became one and a half bottles of gin on weekdays and over the weekends there were two bottles. This was nothing to trumpet about. He continued to lead or rather exist in a wretched life.

This was the scenario every weekend and holiday. His mind was always desperately pining for that bottle of gin. ***Why was it Blue Riband Gin?***

Somehow in the cranny corner of his mind, he thought gin did not stink. Gin is euphemistically referred to as a lady's drink, but the stuff has almost forty per cent alcohol in it.

By divine grace, the official establishment seemed to tolerate his aberrations.

His wife's patience was now running thin with their constant sparring over things minor to something more vexed. At this juncture his octogenarian grandmother suggested the family pay obeisance at the Hanuman temple at Salasar and Radhaji's temple at Merta Road.

His grandmother remained a queen all her life with long ears studded with diamonds, who advised him to religiously recite the *Hanuman Chalisa* with immense devotion to overcome negative thoughts, combat the demons in his mind, and eschew drinking. For once, he listened to some sagacious advice and kept a copy of the *Hanuman Chalisa* and began reading it seriously.

While he was smirked and scorned at by colleagues and by "friends" for compulsive drinking, they were taken aback when Anil Sharma and Tinu Verma (makers of the blockbuster *Gadar*) sauntered into his chamber with customary *filmy* swagger to work out the logistics of filming the climax scene of the Sunny Deol-Amisha Patel starrer which was shot on Lalgarh–Kolayat section of Bikaner division.

Despite the visits to Salasar and Merta Road, his mind remained centred on quotidian drinking.

A few months later the duo of his wife and daughter happened to watch some melodious *bhajans* rendered by a group of bright looking faces, shimmering with serenity. They were buoyed with the energy on display.

His daughter danced with gay abandon to the rhythmic beat of the bhajan, "Gori gori gayan, gore gore gwaal, beech mein mere

madan gopal, Ghas khaye gaiyya, doodh peeye gwaal, maakhaan khaye mero madan gopal."

The songs had an electrifying impact on everyone in the family as they all tapped their feet in unison. There was a magical quality about the *bhajan* which enraptured them.

Unknown to them, this was the second time they were exposed to the Art of Living, for it was only much later that they learnt that the *satsang* they had so enjoyed was conducted by the Art of Living. Some years earlier, Ravi's wife had purchased a cassette of melodious songs (actually Bhajans), which was an Art of Living product. On both the occasions, she was unaware about the foundation called the Art of Living.

His mother spent considerable time practicing Vipassana, Pranic Healing, and Siddha Healing processes which she had learned. She practiced them unflinchingly as it provided her succor and armed with the techniques she passed on curative and positive energy on him through distance healing.

These breathing and other holistic techniques had cured his mother and it was her deep faith that the Universe and the superior intelligence would one day cure him of the ailment of alcoholism.

She was to tell him, "Goenkaji an Indian based in Burma used to have severe attacks of migraine which he countered by using opium injections. However, through the technique of Vipassana he overcame the medical problem."

"What exactly is Vipassana?" was his question next.

"Vipassana, which means to see things as they really are, is one of India's most ancient techniques of meditation. It was taught in India more than 2,500 years ago as a universal remedy for all ills. One just has to observe the breath and upon completion of the ten-day course radical changes happen in the mind and body and several physical ailments get cured through the power of breath.

"Over the years he realized that not only faith, but even breath could move mountains. It is a robust power house about which we are unaware," she added. She suggested that he undertake the ten-day Vipassana course to combat the problem of alcoholism.

However, on account of Operation *Parakram*, he could not leave the place of work and had to be confined to the control office. ***For Ravi, this was a mere ruse to continue with his drinking.***

Meanwhile, his father encountered an unusual experience at Bikaner. One evening during his his customary walk, from nowhere appeared a stranger who tapped his shoulder and remarked, "Ask your son to enroll for the Art of Living course and learn the unique rhythmic breathing technique of Sudarshan Kriya. He will recover from the problem of alcoholism."

This was something inexplicable... And his father was in a state of daze after his brush with this stranger.

This was the only engagement his father had with the stranger. Who was that person? Where did he surface from? How was he aware about his son's vice? All these questions troubled the scientific and logical mind of Ravi's father.

"What is Art of Living? And what is Sudarshan Kriya?" his father was to ask Ravi's mother and wife, who expressed their ignorance.

As spring had set in and Bikaner had warmed up considerably, his parents were now leaving back to Hyderabad.

"This is our last visit to Bikaner, Lakshmi. If Ravi continues to drink this way, we will never visit you," his mother firmly conveyed the message to Ravi's wife.

Providential Transfer to Jaipur

The troops after a year's stay at the frontiers returned back to their barracks and a semblance of normalcy returned between the two warring countries.

Anyway, for the better or the worse Ravi was transferred to Jaipur. His wife recalled the chance dalliance between his father and the stranger at Bikaner and registered his name for the Part 1 course of the Art of Living at Jaipur which was organized very near his house. The die was cast and she was hopeful that something positive would emerge. ***She appeared to have immense faith that a miracle may occur.***

This was something inexplicable and venturing into an unknown turf as Ravi's wife remembered the number of times, they had rendezvous with the name Art of Living cropping up in one way or another without their knowledge. The family was on a learning curve on an uncharted territory.

Women it is believed have greater skill sets, to manage/ handle pain better and are also emotionally and mentally stronger and more robust unlike their male counterparts.

His wife was no different as she drove a somnolent and languorous man to attend the Part 1 course of Art of Living and picked him up every morning after dropping the children at their school. It was a challenging task, but she followed the regimen unflinchingly.

He did not know it at that time but that was to be the first day of the rest of his life.

He was extremely fidgety, sweating in the cold winter of Jaipur in the month of November, stinking of cigarettes and liquor. The teacher and guide scanned through his form and gave him a warm smile.

He was to see a large portrait of a bearded person, who looked beatific and sported an impish smile which could disarm anyone, perched on a mantelpiece as mellifluous music was played in the background. They all were asked to sway to the music and he was quite unsteady on his feet much to the discomfiture of other participants.

It was tough undergoing the course and there were times he wanted to quit. But the teacher encouraged him gently to continue with the course and so did his wife who goaded him not to abandon the ship midway. And then came the earth-shattering moment when the participants were to learn the unique rhythmic breathing technique called the "Sudarshan Kriya".

Zillions of toxins were expatriated from Ravi's body and the stress that had accumulated in trillions of cells in his very being were expunged as he inhaled and exhaled to the syllable of SOHAM (I AM THAT) which was played from a cassette recorder.

It was paced as slow, medium, and fast rhythmic breathing successively, but each breath permeated into each and every cell of Ravi's being. The participants were to listen to the sounds of shrieking, moaning, groaning, and crying as they inhaled and exhaled to the sound of SOHAM. "What was the sound – a mantra, a syllable, a sound…?" They just could not fathom but continued inhaling and exhaling rhythmically.

It was a blast as the entire body ached, and finally collapsed as he shed copious tears and slept like Rip Van Winkle.

This technique was taught over two days and when Ravi met his boss who was quite skeptical about Babas, gurus, rishis, sadhus, swamis, and spiritual masters, he remarked, "Hey you look so fresh. Looks like you have not drunk over the last two days. Quite a feat young man," he added.

But that was not true, he had drunk like a fish, but the breathing technique of Sudarshan Kriya was so overpowering that it eclipsed all negativity and his skin was shining like a star in the firmament. For once he lived up to his name - Ravi.

Upon completion of the course that Sunday, he rang up his mother and could discern palpable happiness and gratitude in her voice. After years, her son had spoken in a sober condition over a weekend.

It is essential that a participant who undergoes the Part 1 course (now called the Happiness Program) should necessarily attend the weekly follow up of Long Sudarshan Kriya apart from practicing the short Sudarshan Kriya every day without fail to derive benefits of the program in its entirety.

It is also sagacious that a participant should also attend various programs from the bouquet of courses designed by Gurudev Sri Sri Ravi Shankar and imparted by the Art of Living Foundation.

Unfortunately, he did neither. And this was a major folly on his part. An Advanced Meditation Course had been planned and had he attended the course right then in 2003, his life would have been so very different.

Golconda and More

It was the faith of his mother in the breathing techniques and other holistic approaches besides prayer proved providential when his wife enrolled him for the Art of Living Part 1 course in Jaipur.

The unique rhythmic became the life boat in trying circumstances and certainly performed a miracle as he could work despite extraordinary addiction to Bacchus.

Humans think, Homo sapiens procrastinate but the cosmos unfolds with immaculate timing which ensures that humans maintain time. His mother always hesitated to call them at Jaipur assuming Ravi would pick up the phone and she would be forced to exchange a few words with a drunken person.

His mother normally never interfered in his transfers and postings. But this time she put her foot on the pedal and pressed the accelerator and sought help from a close family friend and former trade union activist, who was also a staunch devotee of Sathya Sai Baba.

It was once again faith and belief which came into play to perform a miracle.

As Ravi stepped out at Secunderabad station sometime past midnight his head was reeling on account of *excessive* consumption of alcohol during their journey from Jaipur to Hyderabad. He scrambled for space, fresh air and was unsteady on his feet much to chagrin and discomfiture of his wife as the coolies who carted their luggage smirked at his hapless condition.

His parents believed ***and were hopeful*** that the change of place would trigger a positive development and in ***anticipation clutched the last straws*** that his star would shine in the land of the Nizams.

A Visit to a Liver Specialist

"I am amazed at how your son is moving around with this fatty liver…. It would be catastrophic if he continues to drink in this manner," two noted hepatologists were to confide in Ravi's father and wife.

Though he was practicing Sudarshan Kriya regularly at home, he was still not attending the weekly follow-ups nor did he participate in any of the courses which are recommended to all who undertake the Part 1 Course of Art of Living.

But it remained an enigma as to how he continued practicing the *homekriya* (or Short Sudarshan Kriya) unflinchingly.

This was a clear manifestation of faith and belief in the power of breath, almost waiting for a miracle to happen.

Why this happened remained a mystery! Ravi's answer to all doctors and liver specialists who examined him was that he practiced Short Sudarshan Kriya every day (despite consuming alcohol), drank plenty of buttermilk, and consumed Liv. 52.

The liver specialists did acknowledge that Sudarshan Kriya appeared to have had an immense therapeutic value and benefits. It did seem to expunge toxins from the body and the cells were rejuvenated by fresh inject of oxygen.

Several medical practitioners agree that this rhythmic breathing technique increases the level of prana or chi, helping it to virtually permeate into each cell of the body. Many studies conducted in AIIMS, NIMHANS and other hospitals only buttressed this point of view.

In the meantime, Ravi's mother gave him her precious treasure—the *Sai Charitra* (the story and miraculous powers of Sai Baba of Shirdi) to ward off the baleful eye and any malefic planets and asked him to read it while travelling to the office and back and whenever he was free.

Much to the delight of his parents and his wife, he remained sober for a few days, till his mind capitulated once again and while returning from work, Ravi started picking up a quarter bottle of gin, which he consumed upon returning home. The quarter very shortly turned into a half and very soon a full bottle and the consumption only grew. But inspite of everything, Ravi continued doing the Sudarshan Kriya every single day.

His mother also gave him a book on Raghavendra Swami, the Dwaita saint of Mantralayam which he kept in his brief case in addition to the *Sai Charitra.*

Though there was no improvement in his quantum of drinking, nevertheless he continued reading the two books and practicing

Sudarshan Kriya.

But days turned into weeks, weeks into months and he continued his dalliance with liquor. Somewhere in between his maternal uncle Vasudeva Rao took him to AA meetings again as he had earlier done Delhi where he was earlier posted.

In Hyderabad he learnt the Serenity Prayer, which Ravi still keeps in his pouch till date as a reminder about how helpless an alcoholic can be or for that matter any addict.

SERENITY PRAYER

"God, grant me the serenity to accept the things I cannot change, courage to change the things I can, and wisdom to know the difference."

But it was positively the practice of Sudarshan Kriya which provided necessary oxygen (prana) to the moribund cells in his body.

During that time, one fine day Ravi was summoned by the Chief Operations Manager of the zone. He hastened to his room after paying another round of obeisance to Lord Venkateshwara and his consorts and swallowing two tablets of Alprax to sooth his frayed nerves to stave off a panic attack.

He looked at Ravi mischievously and in a stern voice announced that he had been transferred to Guntakal as Senior Divisional Operations Manager on the express orders of the General Manager, and that he had to pack up his bags and leave for Guntakal post haste.

"Take your family along with you, so that you do not feel lonely. Work hard, get immersed in freight operations and not in liquor," barked his benefactor, the Chief Operations Manager of South-

Central Railway.

It was a challenging task and they opined as he would be occupied with work over a period of time, he would give up drinking.

A few months later he was once again transferred back to Hyderabad as his consumption of excessive alcohol was not tolerated by the establishment.

Once back in Hyderabad in a horribly drunken stupor and he found himself in a scrap outside the Chief Minister's Bungalow on Banjara Hills with the cops.

A few hours earlier, he had a *tete-a-tete* with the Chief Operations Manager and that was followed by a lengthy discussion with their family doctor where Ravi was certainly not sober. She concluded that he required psychiatric attention to grapple with the problem of alcoholism. He was taken to a psychiatrist and was now garrisoned so to speak, in a rehab center.

And as the mind was in an obfuscated state his thought process was not straight and it became wild.

Once out of the bars of the rehabilitation center he finally consulted a psychiatrist who prescribed a regime of medication.

He was soon under a treatment of a psychiatrist to overcome the dependency on alcohol. But this had a partial effect as he continued with unabated drinking.

It was not long that his liver and abdomen eventually caved in. First, he suffered from a bout of jaundice and soon developed severe problem of fistula for which he had to be operated upon.

*****

Ravi recalls the events vividly. It was in November 2006 to be exact, that he began having apparitions of Gurudev Sri Sri Ravi Shankar, Raghavendra Swamy and Sathya Sai Baba virtually every day for a

month exhorting him to give up alcohol.

Now these are things which a rationalist, an atheist, and in particular science would ridicule, but he kept wondering as to why was it happening.

Then the penny dropped; a miracle occurred on 9th of December. The family were to leave for Delhi that morning by A.P. Express to attend the wedding of his brother-in-law, slated for 14th of December and he was having a few swigs from the bottle.

Ravi's usually ***calm and self-effacing wife suddenly assumed the incarnation of Goddess Durga*** and snatched the bottle from his hand and severely berated and admonished him.

"This was the tipping point in his life. Number 9 is considered extremely auspicious for Indians especially among Hindus," - so he opined.

And that's it. Ravi had quit drinking, the grace of Gurudev working its magic.

Upon quitting drinking, he recalled attending a mega Advanced Meditation Course of Andhra Pradesh in the year 2007. Gurudev Sri Sri Ravi Shankar met all the participants. Ravi broke down and thanked Gurudev for pulling him out of the morass that he had been sucked into.

So did another youngster who was seated beside him, from the tech field. They were unknown to each other, yet by a strange coincidence happened to be sitting together at Vishalakshi Mantapam (at the Art of Living International Centre, Bangalore).

Interestingly, they both had emerged from alcohol dependency and were at the feet of the Master. This is what Gurudev does when a person surrenders all problems and botherations to him in no uncertain terms.

Gurudev asked Ravi to share his story with the whole world to motivate them to take to adopt this path of happiness.

And miraculously by the spiritual master's grace, several railway men have done the course across the length and breadth of this country with astonishing benefits. There are testimonials of engine drivers giving up smoking, drugs, and alcohol. Ravi was associated in organizing and conducting the courses upon becoming a faculty of Art of Living Foundation.

Similarly, loco pilots who could barely sleep and only sighted signals (red, amber, and green) in their dreams, began to enjoy a sound night's sleep.

This was videographed by a former Divisional Railway Manager (DRM) of Trichy. Similarly, the office staff of DRM, Bangalore, had undergone a lung function test. Smokers, who had participated in the Part 1 course of the Art of Living, were surprised to observe there was no trace of tobacco in their system unlike smokers who did not participate in the program.

In February 2014, Ravi travelled with Gurudev by a special train—*Sri Sri Express. Anugraha Yatra* travelled across the then undivided Andhra Pradesh.

The moment they crossed Kurnool, Gurudev gave Ravi *prasadam* from Mantralayam. He was taken aback and was reminded of an incident at Rayar's Mutt (Raghavendra Swami's mutt), where he had carried liquor into the holy precincts.

During the sanctified Navaratri pujas, photographs taken by advanced cameras are able to capture the extraordinary presence of celestial beings when Gurudev, the Siddha Purush was in deep meditation and the Master slips into ecstasy seeing them.

It is inexplicable and almost unbelievable to an ordinary individual. One must see Gurudev being transported to the seventh heaven, only a Siddha

Purush or a Guru can be in such a state. And one is really blessed and fortunate to witness the Master is such Bhav.

A devotee always pines for the Divine. He or she may not be fully pure. But divinity is so pristine which ignores all shortcomings and also pines for the devotee, however distracted he or she may be.

A pure devotee will certainly witness the Divine form, but that is not to say a devotee who may hanker for material gains would receive blessings (Anugraha) as Almighty God or Divine longs for a disciple or a devotee. This is a secret which lies in the womb of the Universe. Divinity and purity lead to playfulness and spontaneity. Only a spontaneous person gets connected to the sublime form.

The Playfulness of Divinity: Humor and Spontaneity

For all the profound wisdom and deep silence that surrounds Gurudev, there is an equally enchanting aspect of his presence—his effortless humor. The master's laughter is infectious, his wit disarming, and spontaneity unmatched. In a world where spirituality is often equated with solemnity, he reminds us that enlightenment is not a burden, but a dance.

There are countless stories of people coming to him weighed down by their problems, only to leave in peals of laughter. Once, a man approached Gurudev with a deeply furrowed brow, clearly distressed. He began to pour out his struggles when Gurudev, with a twinkle in his eye, simply asked, **"Did you have breakfast?"** The man, taken aback, nodded. **"Good! Then half your problems are already solved."** The unexpectedness of the response made the entire gathering burst into laughter, and in that lightness, the man realized—perhaps his troubles were not as immense as he thought.

In another instance, during a meditation retreat, a devotee stood up and, in all seriousness, asked, **"Gurudev, what is the secret to staying young forever?"** Without missing a beat, he replied with a smile, **"Don't tell anyone your age!"** The room erupted in laughter, but beneath the humor lay a subtle wisdom—age is often more about the state of mind than the passing of years.

During a gathering, a young man stood up and said, "Gurudev, I want to reach enlightenment!" Gurudev chuckled and responded, "Why the hurry? Are you running late for something?" The room burst into laughter, and the seeker himself relaxed, realizing that his pursuit of enlightenment had been filled with unnecessary tension.

Another devotee, known for his strict and disciplined nature, approached Gurudev with a solemn expression. Gurudev simply looked at him and said, "You've forgotten how to smile, haven't you?" The devotee was taken aback but soon found himself laughing for the first time in years. Such is the magic of Gurudev's presence—effortlessly bringing joy where it was long forgotten.

Even in the gravest of situations, Gurudev finds a way to bring lightness. Once, after a long and intense discourse on karma, a devotee anxiously asked, **"Gurudev, what if I have really, really bad karma?"** Gurudev chuckled and said, **"Then make sure you have really, really good dessert."** The entire hall exploded in laughter. The lesson? No matter what has happened, don't carry the weight of the past—learn, move forward, and don't forget to enjoy life's sweetness.

There have been moments when people—rigid in their skepticism or burdened by life's seriousness—have found themselves unexpectedly softened. A corporate leader, known for his strict demeanor, once came to meet Gurudev, expecting a deep intellectual conversation. Instead, within minutes, he found himself laughing like a child at Gurudev's playful banter. Later, he confessed, **"I haven't laughed like this in years. I came here for wisdom, but I think I found something even greater—joy."**

This is the magic of Gurudev. He dissolves years of seriousness not through lectures, but through presence, playfulness, and love. He reminds us that spirituality is not about escaping life—it is about embracing it fully, with laughter and lightness in every step.

A Glimpse into the Beyond: Merging into Peace

In Gurudev's presence, many have described an inexplicable stillness—a silence so powerful that it feels more profound than any spoken wisdom.

A man who had never meditated before found himself attending a program. As he sat near Gurudev, he suddenly entered a deep meditative state, without effort or understanding. "It was as if I was floating in an ocean of peace," he subsequently shared. "I had never felt anything like it before."

Another devotee, struggling with years of inner restlessness, found his mind suddenly empty of thoughts in Gurudev's presence. "It was not emptiness in a negative sense," he explained. "It was a fullness beyond words."

The Ever-Flowing Grace: Experiences Across the World

The presence of a true Master transcends all boundaries of geography, culture, and language. Across continents, from bustling cities to remote villages, people have shared stories of inexplicable moments of grace in Gurudev's presence. His aura does not belong to any one place—it is universal, touching the hearts of seekers regardless of their background.

One such story beautifully exemplifies the spontaneity of his grace. A few years ago, on a pleasant day, Gurudev was traveling in a car with a devotee driving him. Suddenly, he said, "I need a tea." The devotee promptly pulled over at a well-known hotel, but Gurudev simply smiled and said, "Not from here." The driver, though puzzled, continued driving and stopped at another place. Again, Gurudev declined. After some more driving, he finally pointed at a small roadside tea shop and said, "From here."

The devotee stepped out and ordered tea. As the shopkeeper prepared it, he shared an emotional story. A few months earlier, a man had come by, bought tea, and then, in an unfortunate turn of events, another person had stolen all the money the shopkeeper had saved in his drawer. "That money was for my family and me to visit the ashram and seek Gurudev's blessings. It was my lifelong dream, but after losing the money, I felt my wish would never come true."

The devotee listened in awe, realizing the significance of what was unfolding. "Come, bring the tea to my Master yourself," he urged. The shopkeeper hesitated, but the devotee assured him, "I take full responsibility. Just go."

As the shopkeeper approached the car, he was overcome with emotion. Gurudev opened the door and smiled at him. The man stood frozen, tears streaming down his face. In that instant, all his longing, all his unspoken prayers, found their fulfillment. Gurudev looked into his eyes and gently said, "All your wishes are taken care of, my dear."

Such stories of grace are not rare. They are a testament to the unseen force that moves through a true Master—an energy that touches hearts, answers silent prayers, and dissolves barriers of time and space. His presence is beyond comprehension; it is something to be felt, not merely understood. Those who have been blessed with his presence know that he does not merely come and go—he stays forever, in the deepest corners of their being, guiding them in ways beyond words.

Reflection & Exercises:

- ➢ Reflect on how the presence of certain people has impacted your energy and mindset.
- ➢ Visualization exercise—imagine the calming presence of a teacher or guide.

Personal Journal Page: Note the changes in feelings or behavior after encounters with inspirational people.

Part 1: The Making of a Master – Early Life and Spiritual Journey

Chapter 4

Childhood and Family Ties

Gurudev Sri Sri Ravi Shankar: A Childhood Foretold by the Stars

Some lives are scripted by destiny, and the birth of Gurudev Sri Sri Ravi Shankar bore celestial signs that whispered of the path he would walk. His father, a scholar of Ayurveda and astrology, had studied the alignment of the stars for decades. When he was blessed with a son on the auspicious occasion of Shankar Jayanti, it was a divine confluence of omens. It was Ramanuja Jayanti when he was named, and thus, his name carried the resonance of the great seers—Ravi Shankar Narayanan. Yet, due to passport regulations, this full name was shortened, leaving the world to know him as Sri Sri Ravi Shankar.

Even as a young child, his demeanor was strikingly different. There was a faraway gaze in his eyes, as if his mind was tuned to a dimension beyond the ordinary. At the tender age of four, he sat in a park, watching other children play, and suddenly declared, ***"People are waiting for me, I must go to them."*** This innocent yet profound statement hinted at a wisdom far beyond his years—an early awakening to the mission that would later unfold in his life.

His father, lovingly referred to as Pitaji, recounted a defining moment in Sri Sri's early education. When he was four, he was sent to a traditional school where a retired master was to teach him. During the first lesson, the teacher performed a brief puja and uttered the first line of the Bhagavad Gita. To her astonishment, young Ravi Shankar responded by reciting the second line. Stunned by his ability to grasp and recall sacred verses, she rushed to Gurudev's home to share her disbelief. But his father, aware of his son's innate wisdom, simply smiled and encouraged her to continue teaching.

By the age of nine, he had immersed himself in the Rigveda, and by fourteen, he had earned a doctorate in Science and the Vedas. His intellectual progress was astonishingly swift. When he was admitted to school, Sri Sri was promoted three times within three hours—moving from the first standard to the fourth in a single day. This acceleration was but a precursor to the swiftness with which he would later touch millions of lives across the globe.

Unlike most children, he was never absorbed in trivial family matters. His conversations at home revolved around deeper thoughts, reflections on life, and the happiness of humanity. His parents, recognizing the distinctiveness of their son, never restricted his intellectual or spiritual freedom. "The teacher often comes in the way of those who learn," his father would say, allowing Sri Sri's mind to soar unfettered.

But amidst his boundless wisdom and spiritual depth, he remained a loving child. One of his fondest memories was of his father's storytelling. Perched on his father's shoulders, he would eagerly ask for a story, a ritual he shared with his sister, Bhanumathi. Over the years, Pitaji narrated over 1,500 stories, weaving the wisdom of the ages into bedtime tales. As Sri Sri grew older, he would recount these same stories to global audiences, offering a fresh, modern interpretation. "What is he saying, and what is Gurudev saying?" people would ask. His father would smile and reply, "They are one and the same."

Sri Sri's philosophy, even in his childhood, was simple yet profound: Happiness is not elusive—it is intrinsic. People struggle because they do not know how to be happy; they only know how to be miserable. He often shared a revolutionary thought: misery is camouflaged happiness. This notion, counterintuitive to many, especially in the West, gradually became a cornerstone of his teachings.

When he later founded The Art of Living, the name itself was a testament to his belief in making life a joyous experience. Initially, it was to be called The Art of Loving, but cultural connotations led to a change. However, the essence remained: Love and Happiness were the true antidotes to corruption and suffering. He always emphasized that corruption is not just an external phenomenon—it begins in the mind. "If the mind is pure, one cannot be corrupted," he would say.

His father recounted a moment after one of Sri Sri's early courses. "You spoke so beautifully. How did you do it?" he asked. To which Sri Sri simply replied, "I don't know. A power spoke through me." That power, that divinely inspired voice, has since touched millions across the globe.

Even later in life, as a revered spiritual master, he remained Pitaji's loving child. The intimate bond of storytelling and wisdom-sharing remained. His core teachings—love, laughter, and a worry-free mind—continue to resonate across cultures. "Haste jao, hasate jao, dukhon ko door bhagate jao," his father would say, summarizing his son's philosophy in three simple yet profound phrases: Keep laughing, make others laugh, and drive away sorrow.

From a child whose birth was marked by cosmic synchronicity to a global humanitarian, Sri Sri Ravi Shankar's journey was written in the stars but lived with boundless love and compassion. And even many years later, as his father would often say, "Though he is a world-renowned guru, he is still my loving child, and my loving master."

As Gurudev Saw Himself

Sri Sri often reflected on his own life with a sense of deep humility and wonder. He saw himself as merely a vessel through which knowledge flowed, never claiming ownership of his teachings. "I am nothing but an instrument," he would say. His childhood, in his own words, was filled with an innate sense of connection to something greater. Even as a child, he would find himself absorbed in silence, as if the universe itself was whispering to him. He often spoke of how, despite excelling in academics, his true calling was to share joy and wisdom with others. "From a very young age, I knew I had to serve. There was no other path for me," he once said.

A Mother's Love and Perception

His mother, a gentle yet strong woman, viewed him as both a divine gift and a source of boundless love. She often spoke of how he would rarely ask for toys or material pleasures; instead, he found joy in the simplest moments of silence and reflection. "He was always a child of devotion," she would say. Unlike most children, he never threw tantrums or demanded things—his contentment lay in observing and absorbing the world around him. "He was born to bring happiness to others," she would often remark, watching in awe as her young son comforted those in distress with a mere touch or a kind word. To her, he was both a son and a spiritual light, illuminating their home with wisdom and love.

Reflection & Exercises:

- Reflect on early family influences that shaped your values.
- Which early experiences shaped the person you are today?

Personal Journal Page: Document a few formative lessons you learned from any member of your family.

Chapter 5

Formative Years

The Journey of Knowledge and Awakening

From an early age, Gurudev Sri Sri Ravi Shankar displayed an insatiable curiosity about both the material and spiritual realms. His education was not confined to merely textbooks, scholastic pursuits, and achievements; rather, it was an expansive exploration of the nature of existence itself. His ability to grasp complex ideas with ease was evident when, at the age of four, he spontaneously recited the second verse of the Bhagavad Gita after hearing just the first. By the age of nine, he had already delved into the profound verses of the Rigveda, absorbing their essence as if reconnecting with a forgotten wisdom.

His academic prowess was equally remarkable. By fourteen, he had earned a Doctorate in Science and Vedic Studies, showcasing his unique ability to bridge the worlds of empirical knowledge and intuitive wisdom. He found no contradiction between scientific discoveries and spiritual insights; rather, he saw them as two sides of the same coin. Science sought to understand creation through observation and analysis, while spirituality offered a direct experience of the same reality through meditation and inner exploration.

His encounters with physics, particularly quantum mechanics, further reinforced his understanding of the interconnectedness of all things. The concept that an observer influences the observed reality resonated deeply with the ancient Indian wisdom that consciousness is fundamental to existence. He often reflected on how modern physics was gradually catching up with what the Rishis of India had intuited thousands of years ago.

As a student, he was deeply interested in the laws governing the cosmos. He saw parallels between the rhythmic cycles of celestial bodies and the subtle energies governing human consciousness. For him, the study of science was not merely about acquiring knowledge but about uncovering the deeper patterns that pervade all of existence.

His early years were marked by spontaneous revelations about the unity of the universe. He perceived no divide between the microcosm and the macrocosm, between the self and the cosmos. This understanding later shaped his teachings, which seamlessly integrated scientific inquiry with profound spiritual wisdom. His journey was not one of choosing between science and spirituality, but rather of seeing them as an intertwined dance leading to a greater truth.

Even as a young child, his perspective on life was something out of the ordinary. He recalled moments of deep introspection and silent observation. He remembered discovering the reality of death in childhood, watching his grandmother sleep at night, fearing that she would stop breathing. This early awareness of mortality led him to watch the breath—a practice that would later become a cornerstone of his teachings on meditation. "Observing the breath is something that started from the very beginning," he reflected.

His school days were filled with experiences that set him apart. He struggled to fit into ordinary conversations about sports or films, often feeling out of place in the mundane discussions of daily life. "Many times, I wondered if I was in the wrong place," he once shared. While his peers played football, he stood still, unable to bring himself to kick the ball. "This leg cannot kick anything, let alone the ball," he would say with a smile.

Libraries fascinated him, yet he often found himself walking among the shelves without picking up a single book. "I would read the names of books and feel as though I already knew what was inside them," he mused. It was as if knowledge was already present within him, waiting to be ***expressed rather than acquired.***

His teachers, too, recognized something special in him. There were moments when they hesitated to punish him, as though an unseen force restrained them. "They would raise their hands to strike, but then they couldn't do it," he recounted. His presence inspired a natural reverence, even in his childhood.

This synthesis of knowledge and experience set the stage for his later work, where he would offer the world not just intellectual insights but practical tools to experience the harmony between the external world and inner consciousness. His life's mission became clear—to guide others towards this realization and to illuminate the path where science and spirituality meet in a symphony of wisdom.

Reflection & Exercises:

➢ Recall a time when science and spirituality intersected in your life.

Personal Journal Page: Record personal insights on curiosity and discovery.

Chapter 6

Becoming Gurudev

The journey from an insightful young boy to a spiritual teacher, leading up to the founding of the Art of Living Foundation.

The Making of a Master: The Journey from Ravi Shankar to Gurudev Sri Sri Ravi Shankar

The journey from an insightful young boy to a revered spiritual leader was not one of mere happenstance but of deep inquiry, relentless learning, and an unwavering call to serve humanity. From a tender age, Ravi Shankar carried within him an intuitive ability and wisdom that set him apart from others. His childhood had already been imbued with an innate sense of spiritual depth and an unquenchable thirst for knowledge, but it was in his youth that his path truly began to unfold, transforming him into the Gurudev whom the world would come to know.

A Scholar with a Seeker's Heart

H. H. Ravi Shankar's early education had been one of remarkable precocity, but even as he pursued formal studies, he sought knowledge beyond the confines of academia. He enrolled in St. Joseph's College in Bangalore, where he studied physics—a subject that fascinated him for its attempts to unravel the mysteries of the cosmos. But unlike his peers, for whom equations and formulas were mere academic exercises, for him, they were pathways and trajectories to a deeper understanding of existence.

Even as he excelled in his academic studies, he felt an increasing pull towards the inner sciences—the wisdom of the ancient Rishis. His spiritual yearning was never in conflict with his intellectual pursuits; rather, they harmonized within him. He saw no contradiction between the laws of physics and the spiritual truths expounded in the Upanishads. In both, he found an unbroken continuity—scientific inquiry sought to measure reality, while spiritual wisdom sought to experience it.

Mentored by a Legend: Sudhakar Chaturvedi

One of H. H. Sri Sri Ravi Shankar's earliest and most profound influences was **Sudhakar Chaturvedi**, a legendary Vedic scholar, Gandhian, and centenarian who had personally witnessed and participated in India's freedom struggle. Known for his photographic memory and unparalleled mastery over the Vedas, Chaturvedi became Ravi Shankar's first teacher.

The young Ravi Shankar would sit at his feet, absorbing ancient wisdom in its purest form. Chaturvedi's vast knowledge was not limited to scriptures; he had lived through history, carrying within him the echoes of Gandhi's nonviolence and the timeless cadence of Vedic chanting. From him, Ravi Shankar imbibed a love for Sanskrit, an appreciation of India's profound spiritual heritage, and a reverence for the continuity of wisdom passed down through the ages.

It was under Chaturvedi's guidance that Ravi Shankar developed a deep-rooted connection to the sacred sounds of the Vedas, an attunement that would later blossom into the powerful meditation techniques and rhythmic breathwork he would bring to the world.

Under the Guidance of Maharishi Mahesh Yogi

His thirst for deeper wisdom led him to his Guru, Maharishi Mahesh Yogi, the legendary spiritual luminary who introduced the world to Transcendental Meditation. Recognizing the brilliance and depth of this young seeker, Maharishi Mahesh Yogi took him under his wing.

Under Maharishi's tutelage, Ravi Shankar immersed himself in the study of the Vedas, meditation, and the subtle mechanics of consciousness. The young disciple traveled with his Guru across India and abroad, absorbing knowledge that spanned both the mystical and the practical.

Maharishi Mahesh Yogi saw in Ravi Shankar an individual who would take spiritual wisdom beyond the confines of ashrams and temples, making it accessible to every human being. He entrusted him with great responsibilities at a young age, allowing him to interact with scholars, saints, and seekers from across the world. This exposure broadened his perspective, strengthening his conviction that spirituality was not a retreat from life, but a powerful tool to enhance and uplift it. Maharishi once remarked, *"Ravi Shankar is a rare being—one who embodies both deep wisdom and boundless compassion. He will carry this knowledge far and wide, bringing light wherever he goes."*

Encounters with Saints and Mystics

As he traveled across India, he met sages, ascetics, and enlightened beings whose very presence radiated peace. He listened to their wisdom, observed their way of life, and realized that truth was not bound by any single tradition or doctrine. Each saint, each teacher, left a unique imprint on his consciousness, further deepening his understanding of the spiritual path. His interactions with these luminaries solidified his belief that the essence of spirituality lay in simplicity, love, and direct experience.

Several saints who met him saw in him an extraordinary presence. A revered Swami once said, "This young man carries the energy of the ancients. He does not just speak wisdom—he lives it." Another mystic, upon meeting him, declared, "He has the glow of one who has walked this path before. He is not new to this journey—he has returned to fulfill an ancient mission."

According to accounts, when a young Sri Sri Ravi Shankar was brought to meet Anandamayi Ma by his Guru Maharishi Mahesh Yogi, she reportedly said that he was like the "Ganga River," signifying that he would bring a cleansing and purifying effect to the world, essentially predicting his future role as a spiritual leader who would spread peace and knowledge widely. This is considered a significant moment in Sri Sri Ravi Shankar's early life, highlighting the high regard Anandamayi Ma held for him.

Among the countless saints he encountered, many recognized the rare wisdom within him. Some saw in him a teacher, others saw a guide. He, however, saw himself as a student—one who was continuously learning from life itself. He would often sit in deep silence, absorbing the subtleties of spiritual experience, allowing the deeper truths of existence to blossom within him.

The Birth of a Vision: The Art of Living

As the years passed, the young Ravi Shankar felt an increasing call to share what he had learned—not as dogma, but as an experiential journey for others to undertake. By the early 1980s, Ravi Shankar had undergone a period of deep silence and inner exploration that would shape the next phase of his life. It was during this time that the Sudarshan Kriya, a transformative rhythmic breathing technique, was revealed to him. This marked the beginning of a global movement that would eventually touch millions.

This marked the turning point in his journey.

He realized that breath was the bridge between body and mind, between the outer and the inner worlds. If people could learn to regulate their breath, they could tap into an infinite reservoir of joy, peace, and vitality. This realization was the seed that grew into The Art of Living Foundation—a global movement dedicated to personal transformation, stress relief, and service to humanity. With boundless enthusiasm, he began teaching this technique to small groups of people. Word spread quickly, and soon, thousands were drawn to his teachings. What set him apart was not just his wisdom, but his ability to make spirituality practical, joyful, and deeply relevant to everyday life.

Becoming Gurudev Sri Sri Ravi Shankar

As his teachings reached more people, reverence for him grew. He was no longer just Ravi Shankar; he had become a guide, a mentor, a beacon of light for those seeking inner peace. No longer just a seeker, he had become a master. The title 'Gurudev' came naturally—bestowed upon him by those who experienced profound transformation under his guidance. It was not a title he sought, but one that emerged organically, reflecting the deep love and reverence people held for him.

Yet, despite this recognition, he remained as humble as ever. To him, he was still a simple seeker, a student of life. He would often say, "I am nothing but an instrument. The divine does its work through me." His teachings transcended religious and cultural boundaries, making spirituality accessible to all. His presence carried an indescribable energy—one that dissolved doubts, uplifted spirits, and illuminated minds.

Thus, the world came to know him not just as Ravi Shankar, but as Gurudev Sri Sri Ravi Shankar—a title that reflected his role as both a revered spiritual teacher and a universal guide. His journey was not about renunciation but about deep engagement with life—spreading wisdom, fostering peace, and igniting the latent divinity within every individual.

A Journey that Continues

The founding of The Art of Living was just the beginning. Over the decades, his work expanded beyond stress-relief programs to humanitarian initiatives, conflict resolution efforts, and peace-building missions. His message remained constant: to serve humanity with love, wisdom, and joy.

From a young boy watching the stars to a global spiritual leader, Gurudev Sri Sri Ravi Shankar's journey is a testament to the seamless union of knowledge and experience, of science and spirituality, of learning and teaching. His life continues to be an inspiration—a reminder that true wisdom is not in accumulation, but in sharing; not in isolation, but in connection with the world.

In the echoes of ancient chants and the discoveries of modern science, in the laughter of *satsangs* and the silence of deep meditation, Gurudev continues to embody the essence of wisdom, compassion, and boundless love—a living bridge between the past and the future, the known and the infinite.

Reflection & Exercises:

- Identify a turning point in life that led to growth or a calling.
- When have you felt compelled to serve or guide others?

Personal Journal Page: Note the steps of your personal transformation.

Part 2: Building the Art of Living Foundation – A Legacy of Love and Transformation

Chapter 7

A Vision Manifested

A Vision Manifested

The Art of Living Foundation stands today as one of the largest humanitarian and spiritual organizations in the world. Its beginnings, however, were as unassuming as a tiny spark that eventually grew into a blazing fire of transformation, touching millions of lives across continents. The story of its inception is a testament to the boundless love, vision, and spiritual prowess of Gurudev Sri Sri Ravi Shankar—a vision that has become a global movement.

The Humble Beginnings

In the early 1980s, Gurudev began his mission from his own home, welcoming seekers drawn to his profound wisdom and radiant presence. These intimate gatherings were filled with soulful conversations, guided meditations, and the seeds of what would later become the structured programs of the Art of Living. The small groups that gathered around him in those days had no idea they were part of something that would one day span the globe.

As more people started coming, the need for a larger space became apparent. With his characteristic humility and unshakable faith, Gurudev set out to find a place that could serve as a sanctuary for seekers from all walks of life. His search led him to the outskirts of Bangalore, where he found a barren piece of land. It was rocky, arid, and seemingly inhospitable, but he saw beyond the limitations of the land—he envisioned a vibrant ashram that would become a beacon of peace and learning.

Building the Ashram – A Divine Marvel

Acquiring the land was just the beginning. The next challenge was developing it into a livable, vibrant spiritual center. Funds were scarce, and resources limited, but Gurudev's grace and the sheer devotion of his early followers made the impossible happen. Every brick, every structure, and every tree planted on the land is a testament to faith and perseverance.

Volunteers from all over came forward to contribute in whatever way they could. Some donated money, while others gave their time, labor, and expertise. Engineers, architects, and laborers—many of whom were deeply touched by Gurudev's teachings—offered their skills to bring his vision to life. People recount stories of how, despite the lack of finances, material arrived just when required, water sources were discovered through sheer determination, and infrastructure was built brick by brick, fueled by devotion.

One of the most miraculous aspects of this journey was the way financial resources flowed in. Without any formal fundraising campaigns, people who experienced transformation through Gurudev's teachings stepped forward to contribute. Some mortgaged their personal assets to ensure the construction continued, while others organized community efforts to raise funds. Every contribution, big or small, carried an intention of love and dedication, making the ashram a labor of devotion rather than just a structure of concrete and bricks.

Sumeru Mantap – The Sacred Seat of Wisdom

Before the ashram blossomed into the serene sanctuary it is today, a single ancient tree stood as a silent witness to the early days of Gurudev Sri Sri Ravi Shankar's teachings. Under its sprawling shade, seekers from all walks of life gathered, eager to absorb his profound wisdom. Here, on the bare earth, with the sky as his canopy, Gurudev shared timeless truths, guiding individuals toward inner transformation and boundless joy.

It was beneath this very tree that the philosophy of the Art of Living took root—where the first waves of knowledge flowed, shaping the foundation of a movement that would touch millions. Conversations that started in the stillness of nature carried the depth of ancient wisdom, yet held a simplicity that made even the most profound truths accessible to all.

Recognizing the sacred energy of this space, Sumeru Mantap was later built as a tribute to these formative moments. Perched atop a small hill, this open-air meditation space exudes an aura of peace and reverence. With its circular stone seating and panoramic view of the ashram, it continues to be a place where seekers come to meditate, reflect, and reconnect with the same vibrations that once resonated under that humble tree.

Even today, the old tree stands tall, revered as a silent custodian of the past—a living testament to the origins of a global spiritual movement. The whispers of those early discourses still seem to linger in the air, reminding all who visit that wisdom, when shared with love, becomes eternal.

The Haven of Peace – Nature's Embrace

What was once a barren expanse of land has blossomed into a sanctuary of serenity, healing, and transformation. **The Art of Living Ashram,** nestled in the lush embrace of nature on the outskirts of Bangalore, now spans over **250 acres** of verdant beauty, infused with an unmistakable aura of peace and spiritual energy.

At its heart lies the **Vishalakshi Mantap,** an architectural marvel that stands as a beacon of wisdom and inner awakening. Designed in the shape of a lotus—symbolizing purity and transcendence—this grand meditation hall is where thousands gather to experience the profound depths of stillness, silence, and spiritual rejuvenation.

The ashram's gardens, waterfalls, and sacred water bodies have been lovingly nurtured by volunteers over the years, transforming the land into a paradise where the soul finds rest. Towering trees sway in harmony with the wind, vibrant flowers bloom in joyous abundance, and the gentle murmur of flowing water soothes the restless mind.

More than just a place of retreat, the ashram is a living, breathing embodiment of *seva* (service), *sadhana* (spiritual practice), and *satsang* (company of truth). It pulsates with the collective energy of seekers from across the world—meditating, chanting, and engaging in selfless service. The air is thick with devotion, the walls echo with laughter, and every sunrise carries the promise of renewal.

Whether one comes seeking solace, wisdom, or simply a moment of stillness, the ashram extends its warm embrace to all, a sacred space where the body heals, the mind quiets, and the spirit soars.

The Vishalakshi Mantap – An Architectural Wonder

Named after Gurudev's mother, the Vishalakshi Mantap is a breathtaking architectural marvel, envisioned and designed by H.H. Sri Sri Ravi Shankar himself. This majestic edifice stands as the spiritual heart of the ashram, radiating serenity and grace. Rising 108 feet into the sky, the structure encompasses five expansive floors and two basements, crowned by a 15-foot-high kalasha—one of the tallest of its kind in Asia.

What sets this extraordinary structure apart is its ingenious engineering. Despite the immense weight concentrated at its center, the Mantap remarkably lacks a central supporting column. Instead, its entire framework is upheld by 81 intricately positioned pillars along the periphery. This groundbreaking design, the result of months of precise structural calculations, masterfully redirects the load from the center to the edges, ensuring both stability and an unparalleled sense of openness. The result is an architectural masterpiece that is as technically sophisticated as it is aesthetically sublime.

More than just a marvel of design, the Vishalakshi Mantap is a sacred space—a sanctuary for deep meditation, transformative *satsangs*, and profound spiritual experiences. The structure's design mirrors the blooming of a lotus, symbolizing purity, enlightenment, and the unfolding of divine wisdom. Seamlessly blending ancient spiritual aesthetics with modern engineering brilliance, it stands as a testament to both vision and devotion, offering all who enter, an atmosphere of peace, grace, and transcendence.

The Power of Transformation

As the ashram began to take shape and blossom so did the lives of those who came seeking solace. The simple breathing techniques and meditative practices that Gurudev introduced became tools for inner transformation. People found healing, not just from stress but from deep-seated traumas and emotional burdens. Stories abound of individuals who arrived with hopelessness in their hearts but left with renewed purpose.

One such story is of a young woman who had lost everything to personal tragedy. She arrived at the ashram in despair, but within weeks of immersing herself in the programs and the serenity of the space, she found a newfound lightness. She went on to become one of the most dedicated volunteers, touching the lives of thousands through her work.

A Global Phenomenon

What began in Gurudev's home soon blossomed into an organization spanning over 180 countries. As the ashram grew, so did the global presence of the Art of Living. Gurudev's tireless travels, his teachings, and his ability to connect with people from all backgrounds brought the message of peace and transformation to millions.

Governments recognized the impact of his work, and soon, Art of Living programs were being introduced in prisons, corporate spaces, and even conflict-ridden regions. Whether it was rehabilitating former rebels in Colombia, providing trauma relief in war zones, or conducting large-scale meditation events that brought together people from diverse backgrounds, the foundation became synonymous with inner and outer peace.

A Living Legacy

Today, the ashram stands as a testament to what faith, love, and dedication can achieve. What was once a barren land is now a lush, thriving sanctuary that has become a pilgrimage site for seekers from all over the world. It is not just a place of learning but of miracles—where questions dissolve, where stress disappears, and where one experiences the sheer joy of being alive.

One of the most significant manifestations of this growth are the Sri Sri Gurukul and the Sri Sri School of Yoga, both established as pillars of education and spiritual practice. These institutions embody Gurudev's vision of creating spaces where holistic education, culture, and well-being are prioritized, not just intellectual growth.

Sri Sri Gurukul

The Sri Sri Gurukul, founded as part of Gurudev's initiative to preserve and promote traditional knowledge, aims to provide children with an education that nurtures the mind, body, and spirit. Located within the serene expanse of the ashram, this Gurukul integrates ancient wisdom with modern learning techniques. It provides students not only with academics but also with a deep understanding of ethics, spirituality, and the importance of service to society. Over the years, the Gurukul has expanded and evolved, offering a curriculum that includes spiritual practices like meditation and yoga, alongside conventional subjects, creating well-rounded individuals who are equipped to serve the world with wisdom and compassion.

Sri Sri School of Yoga

Similarly, the Sri Sri School of Yoga has been a beacon for those seeking a deeper connect with themselves through the transformative power of yoga. Founded to offer an authentic education and knowledge in the yogic sciences, the school has attracted students from all over the world. It offers a variety of courses that focus not just on physical postures (asanas) but also on breathing techniques (pranayama), meditation, and the science behind these practices. Gurudev often quotes the *Patanjali Yoga Sutras* and *Yoga Vashishtha*. He says, "Yoga for physical hygiene and meditation for mental hygiene."

Students are trained to become instructors, sharing their newfound wisdom with communities across the globe. What began as a small initiative has now expanded to multiple locations worldwide, with thousands of certified teachers imparting the benefits of yoga to millions.

Sri Sri Wellbeing and Ayurveda Hospital

In line with Gurudev's holistic approach to life, Sri Sri Wellbeing was established to provide individuals with a sanctuary for physical, mental, and emotional healing. The center integrates the wisdom of Ayurveda, an ancient system of healing, with modern wellness techniques. Alongside wellness retreats, the Sri Sri Ayurveda Hospital, part of the wellbeing initiative, has become a global sanctuary for those seeking respite from chronic illnesses, stress, and ailments that conventional medicine often struggles to address.

The hospital and wellness center are designed to provide an environment of serenity and healing, surrounded by lush greenery, peaceful landscapes, and an atmosphere that nurtures the soul. People from across the globe travel to the center to rejuvenate themselves through Ayurvedic treatments, yoga therapy, and stress-relief programs. The peaceful ambience, combined with the therapeutic approaches has helped thousands find healing and renewal.

Transformation of the Ashram Landscape

The metamorphosis of the ashram is nothing short of miraculous. From the very beginning, Gurudev envisioned the ashram not only as a space for learning and meditation but also as a sanctuary of nature, where visitors could feel connected to both themselves and the Earth.

Now a vibrant, verdant landscape, brimming with flowering

plants, towering trees, and peaceful gardens, this living, breathing ecosystem has become a pilgrimage site for seekers from all over the world. Each step within the ashram grounds brings one closer to a sense of inner peace, with the gentle sounds of nature enhancing the tranquility.

Gurudev has often spoken of nature as a mirror to the mind, and the landscape of the ashram is designed to reflect this principle, with every tree and flower symbolizing a step toward serenity. The air itself seems to be infused with an aura of peace, offering respite to those who seek a space for spiritual nourishment. Visitors come here not only to learn but to experience something far greater—a reconnection with themselves and the world around them.

The Dhyan Mandir: From Yagya Shala to a Temple of Peace

The transformation of the Yagya Shala into the Dhyan Mandir is another important chapter in the development of the ashram. The Yagya Shala, which was originally designed for Vedic fire ceremonies, was a sacred space where devotees would gather to offer their prayers and perform rituals. However, as the needs of the community grew, Gurudev envisioned a larger, more expansive space that could accommodate the ever-growing number of spiritual seekers who were coming to the ashram. This vision led to the construction of the Dhyan Mandir.

The Dhyan Mandir, currently under construction, is designed to be a majestic space where people can gather for meditation, prayer, and reflection. Unlike any typical temple, it is a place dedicated not only to spiritual practice but to deep inner silence. It is a space that allows individuals to quiet the mind and connect with their inner divinity. With its architectural beauty, serene atmosphere, and profound energy, the Dhyan Mandir is poised to become a new center of global spiritual activity and peace.

Gurudev's Legacy: A Celebration of Life

As we look at the growth of the ashram and the myriad initiatives it has spawned, we realize that Gurudev's legacy is not merely in the physical buildings, but in the transformation of countless lives. The ashram is a living testament to his teachings: that life is a celebration. The programs, the teachings, and the initiatives have all been designed with one goal in mind—to offer people the tools to experience the joy and peace that comes from connecting with their true selves.

Gurudev's words, ***"Life is a celebration,"*** have become the guiding light for millions of people who have been touched by his teachings. Through the Art of Living, individuals are empowered to experience life as a celebration of love, peace, and joy. The teachings go beyond just theory; they provide practical tools that allow people to bring peace, harmony, and balance into their everyday lives.

Not just in Bengaluru, his ashrams are spread across the world providing and being a haven of peace for millions.

The journey of the Art of Living Foundation continues, a testament to the power of one man's vision to bring peace, happiness, and a true celebration of life to every corner of the world.

Celebrations continued unabated in the Divine Aura of Gurudev Sri Sri Ravi Shankar in the form of two Rail Yatras along with the Master. One in Andhra Pradesh and the other in Uttar Pradesh.

Spiritual Odyssey With The Master -

Sri Sri Express — Anugraha Yatra in Andhra Pradesh

(15 to 19 February 2014)

In ancient India, Kings performed the Ashwamedha Yagya to expand their kingdoms through forcible conquests or else states accepted the suzerainty and became vassals. Gurudev undertook a cultural conquest spread over five days and won the hearts of the people through Divine love. The horse was replicated by a train.

This train consisting of 20 coaches including a saloon meant for Gurudev was christened the Sri Sri Express (Anugraha Yatra). The journey covered 18 districts of the former state of Andhra Pradesh, where Gurudev interacted with lakhs of people. Four major *satsangs* were held at Produttur, Tirupati, Mangalgiri and at the coastal town of Kakinada. Further he mingled enroute at several stations with thousands of devotees. The Yatra commenced at Kacheguda, Hyderabad on 15 February.

It would be a fair statement to make that Mahatma Gandhi had undertaken a similar journey by rail, crisscrossing the countryside, spreading the message of peace, non-violence, evils of consumption of alcohol and communal harmony besides exhorting people to take up cudgels against the tyrannical British rule. This Yatra too was reminiscent of the journey undertaken by the Mahatma. This was mentioned by those 'frail in body but strong in spirit' senior citizens or offspring of those who had witnessed the earlier event during the course of the journey especially in the interior portions of Andhra Pradesh.

A Background

A chilly and wintry morning greeted us in Bangalore sometime in 2010. As part of Ravi's protocol duty, along with other senior railway officials he received the Gurudev Express (a special train commemorating the 150th birth anniversary of Rabindranath Tagore) at Bangalore Cantonment Station. There was a fleeting thought in

his mind that, had Gurudev Sri Sri Ravi Shankar been the chief guest of the function, the headlines and breaking news would have been *GURUDEV RECEIVES GURUDEV*. The seed of this sui generis train (really one of its kind), the Sri Sri Express was thus sown.

Promptly, a mail was sent to Gurudev to travel by a special train in Karnataka, showcasing various facets of the Art of Living, particularly the breathing technique of Sudarshan Kriya and various *seva* activities of the NGO.

Some tentative plans were chalked out to run a train, on the lines of the Deccan Odyssey or the Palace on Wheels. However, perhaps the time was not ripe, and the mission was aborted.

Meanwhile, Ravi was transferred to South Central Railway, and along with Kishoreda (an Advanced Meditation Course Teacher and among Gurudev's first disciples) kept requesting the Master to allot dates and travel Andhra Pradesh by a special train.

But a mere request is not answered unless accompanied by a deep *sankalpa*. It needs to be supported by a concrete action plan. Gurudev was scrutinizing our seriousness and determination. A sincere prayer in the heart along sincerity in our action, besides maintaining humility and devotion is mandatory.

Along the way, Kumar from the Railways, Mani Naidu, a devotee and an entrepreneur, and Ravi Bhaiyya, a very senior Art of Living teacher from Hyderabad, Vaishali Venkat (the then State Teacher's Coordinator), Vani Bala (media coordinator) and Chitra Ananth (a teacher), all joined the organizing team and we kept persisting with the proposal. From 2011 to 2012 the team of Art of Living, Andhra Pradesh kept a fervent request letter at the sanctum sanctorum during the Shivaratri and Navratri Pujas seeking Divine blessings, hoping that Gurudev would give his nod.

Finally, Gurudev, at a Teachers' Refresher Meet, agreed to the dates sometime in February 2014. Some of the organizers were overcome by anxiety and feverishness which literally forced Guruji to advance the programme to November 2013. However, there was an unanticipated poor response in bookings, inclement weather conditions, and the agitation by the populace of Seemandhra against the bifurcation of Andhra Pradesh. The Guru was aware of all but gave a long rope and in all his magnanimity altered the dates to the earlier planned February 2014. The superconscious mind had all along known the dates, but the ordinary mortal and his mind did not comprehend the cosmic divine plan.

During the course of this historical Yatra, Sri Sri addressed four major *satsangs* and several station-side meetings. Our present-day politicians, who roister in road side shows, should have witnessed the fervor of the faithful and the casual onlooker at the stations where the Sri Sri Express was provided a scheduled or an unscheduled halt. The entire thrust of Gurudev was a campaign against an unjust bifurcation of Andhra Pradesh (keeping the sentiments of Seemandhra in mind), forcible proselytization and the need for good governance not only in Andhra Pradesh but in the country as a whole. Gurudev skillfully and succinctly raised these issues during the entire Yatra without offending any particular group's feelings or sentiments.

Gurudev is an amazing wordsmith and at all *satsangs* his simple message was that we keep changing our Gods and not the guards (leaders) who administer us. By changing Gods neither are we devoted to any faith but also betray our ancestors. Further, by constantly reposing faith in the same guards (political leaders), the wheels of growth and development get fossilized and do not provide succor to the hapless population. Thus, the need to vote for a better India. He was quite candid in mentioning that Lord Krishna could have comfortably played the flute for the Gopas and Gopikas of Brindavan, but plunged into politics to uphold *Dharma.*

Before the Sri Sri Express embarked upon the historical tour, several roadblocks and knots were cleared by the grace of the Master. So much so that Railways provided the Art of Living with concession even though it was a commercial project as far as railways was concerned. To begin with there were only a few of us involved in this 'Yagya'. Unfortunately, the organizing team was trapped in the vortex of ego and Gurumandal.

Gurudev purged it all by his grace, and thus a larger group was formed to execute the project. During the course of the preparation, the AP Apex Body astutely led by Shri Ramachandranji and Shri Ravi Kumar formed select committees to keep an eagle's eye on each aspect of the project. These pertained to marketing, catering, logistics and operations, hotel arrangements, publicity et al.

Day 1

Kacheguda to Yerraguntla

A special train consisting of 10 sleeper coaches, 6 air-conditioned coaches, a pantry car, saloon for Gurudev and guard's van rolled into Kacheguda station of Hyderabad. More than 1,000 spiritual travelers awaited Gurudev's arrival with a bated breath. He was greeted with a Nadaswaram recital and literally floated to his saloon. The faithful could hardly believe their eyes and jostled with each other to have a glimpse of the Master.

The Sri Sri Express (Anugraha Yatra) stopped at Mehboobnagar, Gadwal, Kurnool Town, Dhone, Gooty, and Tadipatri before reaching Yerraguntla. Thousands flocked to have a glimpse of the Master. He was accorded a traditional welcome and people could scarcely believe that Gurudev was amidst them and speaking on esoteric subjects like spirituality, pranayama, dhyana, yoga, and topical subjects like bifurcation of the state, voting for a better and a robust India, and perils of alcoholism among others.

Gurudev, who is pure energy personified, sprang surprises on the passengers by boarding the train and meeting each and every devotee, celebrating their birthdays, cutting cakes, garlanding those who had their anniversaries and so on, while commiserating with their problems if any and primarily making them happy. Devotees were dumbstruck that Gurudev like any ordinary traveler, was traversing through the 20 coaches of the train. This is what they yearn for; this is what they pine for—to have a glimpse of the Master. Each and every traveler opined that they had never had such an interaction with Gurudev ever in their lives.

He interacted with the security personnel and the cooks of the pantry car. With remarkable prescience, Gurudev mentioned that Indian Railways ought to have air-conditioned pantry cars in trains so that the food cooked does not get contaminated in any manner. His concern about the quality of food being provided to both nationals and internationals was indeed touching, as he does in the kitchen of the Art of Living Ashram.

As the sun sank at Yerraguntla, and shadows lengthened, the train chugged into the station. The IRCTC (Indian Railway Catering and Tourism Corporation) which was not only providing security and food, arranged buses to ferry passengers to Prodottur, where the first of the four *Mahasatsangs* were organized in the trip. Even though the train was running behind schedule, a record crowd had turned up for the *satsang*, where Gurudev conducted a meditation session and spoke with effortless felicity and ease, which perhaps only he can.

In that quiet recognition, something settles—leaving behind not answers, but a deeper knowing.

Day 2

Renigunta to Tirupati

Sri Sri Express arrived early in the morning at Renigunta on the 16th. Gurudev (Narayana) had left early in the morning for Tirumala and freshened up at Padmavati Guest House and then he was received by Shri Bappi Raju (MP and then Chief of Tirumala Tirupati Devasthanam). He meditated and was present during the Suprabhata Puja. What a mirror image of Narayana performing puja to the Lord! At the crack of dawn, with a slight drizzle and incandescent bulbs still glowing provided the setting of Vaikuntha.

Gurudev was felicitated by the priests of Tirumala with Vedic hymns and incantations reverberated through the temple. Meanwhile, 1,000 devotees travelling on the special train got ready in various hotels at Tirupati and reached Tirumala. Vaishali, the State Teachers Coordinator of AP, along with a senior bureaucrat, made arrangements for the Darshan of Lord Venkateswara. It was quite a task to ensure that all devotees went in a group for the

Darshan. Gurudev had other plans. He conducted a meditation for 1,000 devotees, before they all could have Lord Balaji's Darshan.

With one stroke, Gurudev ensured the presence of all the devotees rather than them going adrift. Corporates and governments alike can learn a few lessons in skillful management of men, material and time. The devotees had never experienced such a powerful meditation or a group Darshan of this nature.

Before the evening *satsang,* Gurudev paid homage at Goddess Padmavati's temple at Tiruchanur, where the incantation of the hymns was meditative and intoxicating.

This was followed by a massive *satsang* at the university grounds. The meditation and bhajans by Shalini and Srinivas held people spellbound. Yes Plus activists enacted the jingle of Rail Yatra... Sri Sri to perfection. The jingle in Telugu which incidentally was the theme song of the Yatra indicating the places where Gurudev would be visiting along with different facets of the Art of Living, a rap song and proper marketing became a very big hit with the devotees and other members of the public.

Day 3

Renigunta to Mangalgiri

On Monday, the organizing team felt that something was amiss. How could the Master not perform the weekly Rudra Puja? Gurudev (Shiva) reached Srikalahasti and was present during the Rahu-Ketu Puja and Rudra Puja, too. As soon as the train reached Srikalahasti, Guruji breezed in and boarded the Sri Sri Express. The devout saw the Divine energy spreading as he entered the saloon.

Guruji touched Nellore, Ongole, Bapatla, Chirala, and Tenali before reaching Mangalgiri. Enroute, he was greeted by enthusiastic crowds and the Master spread the divine knowledge and his deep concern to make India a strong country. There are very few spiritual leaders who make such a strong pitch, not only to rejuvenate the country spiritually but also politically. He has no stakes. His only mission is to spread the gospel of truth and purity. In fact, Gurudev is the Supreme Consciousness. He is purity, hollow and empty, sacred; he symbolizes Narayana and Shiva-Shakti.

This energy made him visit each coach several times a day and alight at every station to address the devotees. On an average, he would have walked around 8 kilometers daily without fail. And with enthusiastic devotees jostling and falling over him, the task was even more arduous and cumbersome.

That evening, a grand *satsang* was organized at a resort called Hailand at Mangalgiri. The grandiose stage did not quite impress the Divinity. He specifically spoke about the need to ensure austerity and simplicity. He was quite candid in mentioning that such backdrops only act as distractions.

The 1,000-odd devotees were housed at Hailand resort and suddenly problems of boarding and lodging cropped up. Gurudev assuaged the devotees by uttering the word 'toilets' in his inimitable trademark style and disarmed all agitation and disquiet from the minds of the faithful. By his grace, despite purported lack of accommodation, every traveler was provided a place to sleep and to freshen up the next morning. It was again the energy and magic of the Master at work.

Day 4

Mangalgiri to Kakinada

While the devotees boarded the train at Mangalgiri, Gurudev performed puja at Narasimha Swamy temple.

Gurudev, in this segment of the journey, stopped at Vijayawada, Gudiwada, Akividu, Bhimavaram Town, Kovvur, Rajamundhry, and finally the train terminated at Kakinada. Thousands flocked to the stations and Gurudev's grace simply flowed. Despite the crowds, the Master walked from one end of the platform to the podium in the circulating area of the station which was at quite a distance.

Like a child, Gurudev transfixed his gaze at the bridge over the Godavari and posed questions about chain pulling, crossing of trains, speed of trains, among others.

The journey culminated at Kakinada where Gurudev addressed a massive gathering. And 108 Grama Devatas of coastal Andhra too were propitiated.

The dream journey culminated on the morning of the 19th at Kacheguda. While one can chronicle the physical aspect of the journey, it is next to impossible to gauge the spiritual energy received by the 1,000 travelers, station staff enroute, staff on board and a few lakh people who saw Gurudev in the physical form. People were transported from the mundane to the sublime in these five days and those memories will be always etched to become better human beings and contribute to society.

The Journey had just begun. The clairvoyant Gurudev had prophesized that a major event would be held in Delhi. This was to be the World Culture Festival at Delhi held in March 2016 where artistes, philosophers, politicians, farmers, corporates and the devout assembled to celebrate "Vasudaiva Kutumbakam."

Om Anugrah Yatra in Uttar Pradesh

A Second Rail Yatra

Some devotees and faculty were aware of the A.P. Rail Yatra and I suggested a similar tour by Gurudev in Uttar Pradesh. They were ecstatic on hearing the proposal.

Om Anugrah Yatra was a singular opportunity to accompany Gurudev Sri Sri Ravi Shankar by train through the bijou towns and vast tracts of agrarian lands of Uttar Pradesh. A special train had been arranged for over 1000 devotees to join Gurudev as he visited several sacred and religious spots, both Hindu and Buddhist.

On 26th of February, 2018 the devotees assembled at Varanasi and had the fortune of visiting Sarnath near Varanasi—the place where Gautama Buddha gave his first discourse. Later in the evening, pilgrims stayed on for the soulful *satsang* and knowledge session.

On the morning of 27th February devotees attended a special *Sant Samagam* in Gurudev's presence once he arrived at Varanasi, the oldest and most sacred cities of the world. In the evening the train reached Gorakhpur – a city in the Buddhist midland where a *Mahasatsang* with Gurudev was held after he had had a meeting with the Chief Minister of the state.

On 28th of February, the travelers visited Shravasti –where Buddha spent his final twenty-four rainy seasons in deep meditation. The journey terminated with a grand *Mahasatsang* at Lucknow on the 28th evening, where Gurudev administered a pledge against taking dowry and violence against women.

There were *darshans* at railway stations en route at Mau, Deoria,

Balrampur and Gonda enabling curious onlookers, farmers and devotees living in rural areas to receive the *Anugrah* or blessings of Gurudev and to promote spirituality, yoga, peace and harmony.

Ravi was indeed fortunate to travel with Gurudev in his saloon both in *Sri Sri Express* and once again during *Om Anugrah Yatra.* He was extremely fortunate and blessed to be in close proximity with Gurudev and see the Master unravelling his divinity. Those are the real precious moments of Glimpses of Grace.

Ravi could not but help think, there are millions of devotees of Gurudev across swathes of lands but he was the only one among all of them to travel in his saloon not once, but twice during the two Rail Yatras. As recently as 2025 when someone mentioned about Rail Yatra to Gurudev, the Master was to refer to Ravi. "Oh, he still recalls." Ravi was choked with emotion and tears welled up his eyes.

During the course of the travel Gurudev had skillfully separated chaff from the grain. Gurudev in his masterly manner assuaged the frayed nerves of the teachers, organizers, and devotees the way only he could. He was to guide Ravi like a shrewd businessman that, while organizing the *yatra* and spreading the message of Art of Living is a yeoman task, one needs to be cost conscious and the organization ought not to suffer in any manner or face the flak in any manner.

A Lesson to be Learnt – Never have a Doubt

The secretariat at Bangalore Ashram was closely monitoring the logistics and were keen to know the places where Gurudev would be staying for the night and as to how the Master would reach the *satsang* venues.

The *Om Anugraha Yatra* Express chugged along from Varanasi to Gorakhpur, albeit delayed, as surging crowds of devotes, curious onlookers, farmers in particular stopped the train to have a glimpse of the Master and seek his blessings.

Gurudev paid special attention to farmers of eastern Uttar Pradesh and desired that SSIAT- the Sri Sri Institute Agricultural Trust continue their programs with gusto and expand the reach. Quite interestingly the moment Gurudev alighted at Varanasi station he gave me a large stalk of a plant gifted to him by a farmer.

Kishoreda who headed SSIAT was very keen that Gurudev interacts with the farmers and had repeatedly mentioned to Ravi that there ought to be no failure on this account.

The Master who is aware about everything thus gave Ravi the stalk only to remind him in a subtle manner that amidst various programs the farmers of U.P. necessarily had to meet Gurudev.

The locale in Gorakhpur was in the railway colony and the organizers opined that Gurudev could have a brief stopover at Ravi's sprawling bungalow, refresh after the journey from Varanasi to Gorakhpur and his meeting with the Chief Minister.

Meanwhile a turf war was going on between anxious, competing devotees about where to house Gurudev during his stay at Varanasi, Gorakhpur, and Lucknow.

Ravi's excitement was palpable and he informed his family members that Gurudev would spend the night at his place before embarking on the journey to Lucknow the following day. All the necessary arrangements were made at the railway bungalow to receive Gurudev.

Yet Ravi kept asking members of the entourage from Bangalore Ashram traveling with Gurudev and his family members as to where would He spend the night. "Look, he is travelling with Gurudev yet he is not sure about anything," his mother would exclaim quite exasperated. "He should surrender totally to the master for miracles to take place and have no doubts."

Upon reaching Gorakhpur, Gurudev headed straight to Gorakhnath Mutt and had a one-on-one meeting with the Chief Minister of Uttar Pradesh, Shri Yogi Adityanath on untangling the vexed issue of Ayodhya temple. If there was one person the sparring parties were willing to listen to, it was none other than Gurudev.

Meanwhile, Gurudev's motorcade waded through the teeming crowds of Gorakhpur and reached the railway rest house where he eventually spent the night.

Despite being dismayed, Ravi mustered the courage and requested Gurudev to visit his home and bless the family.

Seeing his plight and fervent appeal, Gurudev agreed to come over on his way to the evening *satsang* at the railway grounds.

The moment he arrived, he garlanded Ravi's father and declared looking at him, "I have come for him and not you." Gurudev was accorded the traditional South Indian welcome. Those present were awestruck as the Master breezed in and out, showering blessings, affection, and love.

Ravi's agnostic, nonagenarian ailing father was absolutely stunned and amazed as the spiritual master garlanded him which instilled a sudden burst of energy.

The following day Gurudev travelled from Gorakhpur to Lucknow and during the period, the highpoint was a meditation session at Shravasti. Gurudev was all joy and radiance and spent quality time at Shravasti and continued with the tradition laid by Buddha thousands of years ago.

A Destination Wedding!

During the yatra a young couple were taken aback when Gurudev solemnized their marriage on the train. Marriages are normally performed at places of worships, marriage halls, and public places to name a few

But this was truly a destination wedding. A dream wedding performed on the train with Guruji performing the role of the chief priest as *pujaris* chanted the Vedic hymns. The ecstatic couple exchanged vows and garlands and more importantly moved around Gurudev rather than the holy fire seeking his blessings. The footage was captured and they were to become almost a celebrity couple as the video was now being shared and watched by thousands across India and the globe as everyone watched it live with disbelief.

Memories of the Rail Yatra lingered in Ravi's mind as he travelled back from Lucknow to Allahabad (by now he had just been transferred to Allahabad).

Soon Ravi was back to work, and allowed the phone to ring incessantly as he kept reliving those golden moments of the yatra which are parked in memory bank forever … waiting to be part of yet another Rail Yatra.

Reflection & Exercises:

- Reflect on your own vision for contribution and impact.
- What small steps today could move you toward a larger purpose?

Personal Journal Page: Make a note of actionable goals inspired by Gurudev's vision.

Chapter 8

The Sudarshan Kriya and Beyond

Sudarshan Kriya and Beyond

At the banks of the serene Bhadra River, in the depths of silence, a profound revelation unfolded—one that would transform millions of lives across the globe. After ten days of deep silence and meditation, Sudarshan Kriya was revealed to Gurudev Sri Sri Ravi Shankar, a breath-based technique that would soon become a cornerstone of spiritual well-being and holistic healing. What emerged from this moment of deep stillness was not just a mere breathing technique but a gift to humanity—one that harmonizes the rhythms of life, detoxifies the system, and awakens the profound depths of inner peace.

The Science and Power of Sudarshan Kriya

Sudarshan Kriya, meaning "Proper Vision through Purifying Action," is a rhythmic breathing practice that aligns the body, mind, and spirit. It incorporates distinct breathing cycles—slow, medium, and fast—that mirror the natural rhythms of life. This dynamic yet simple practice has been the subject of extensive scientific research, with studies highlighting its impact on stress reduction, emotional well-being, and overall health.

Research conducted at prestigious institutions, including Harvard Medical School, the All India Institute of Medical Sciences (AIIMS), and the National Institute of Mental Health and Neurosciences (NIMHANS), has shown that Sudarshan Kriya significantly reduces cortisol levels, the stress hormone, while simultaneously increasing levels of prolactin, the well-being hormone. It enhances autonomic nervous system balance, improves heart rate variability, and fosters deep emotional resilience. Studies have documented its efficacy in alleviating symptoms of anxiety, depression, PTSD, and even chronic health conditions such as hypertension and insomnia.

But beyond scientific validation, Sudarshan Kriya has been a beacon of transformation for millions. From war-torn regions to corporate boardrooms, from prison inmates to world leaders, individuals from all walks of life have experienced the profound shift that this practice brings.

Beyond Sudarshan Kriya: The Profound Meditative Journeys

While **Sudarshan Kriya** remains the cornerstone of the Art of Living's transformative programs, Gurudev Sri Sri Ravi Shankar has designed a **multifaceted spiritual path**, integrating a vast array of ancient and contemporary techniques that guide seekers beyond breathwork—into deeper states of meditation, awareness, and self-realization. His vision is to make **timeless wisdom and profound meditative experiences accessible to all**, regardless of background, belief, or prior experience.

The Science of Effortless Meditation

Each meditation technique introduced by Gurudev serves a distinct purpose, addressing different aspects of human consciousness and well-being:

✧ **Sahaj Samadhi Meditation** – A mantra-based meditation that effortlessly takes the mind into profound stillness and deep rest. Unlike meditative practices requiring intense concentration or effort, Sahaj Samadhi allows one to dive naturally into an expansive state of awareness, where stress dissolves and inner joy unfolds.

✧ **Vigyan Bhairav** – Rooted in the esoteric wisdom of Kashmir Shaivism, this ancient compendium of 112 powerful meditation techniques offers a gateway to transcendence. These are believed to be meditation techniques that Lord Shiva taught Goddess Parvati. Gurudev has revived and made these practices accessible, allowing modern seekers to experience the pure awareness and boundless presence that sages have explored for millennia.

The teachings of Vigyan Bhairav, rooted in the ancient Shiva Sutras, provide an array of techniques for exploring consciousness beyond thoughts. Participants have reported spontaneous moments of deep awareness, heightened intuition, and an effortless connection to the present moment.

✧ **Sanyam** – A profound, immersion-based retreat where silence, meditation, and heightened awareness converge. This advanced program enables participants to observe the finest layers of consciousness and experience expanded states of perception beyond the ordinary mind. Several rounds of Padma *Sadhana* are performed, and the program is conducted in two levels: Sanyam 1 and Sanyam 2. One can see the resplendent look on the faces of the devotees/seekers who have undertaken the course.

Holistic Programs for Inner & Outer Transformation

Gurudev's teachings are not limited to meditation alone. He has curated a diverse range of holistic well-being and self-development programs, blending wisdom, breath, yoga, and deep meditative techniques to awaken human consciousness to expand the potential of the human mind.

✧ **The Art of Silence Course** – A retreat where participants delve into deep silence and self-inquiry, discovering insights and inner peace beyond words.

✧ **Prajñā Yoga** – A unique combination of yogic postures and meditative techniques that align the body and mind, fostering mental clarity and emotional balance.

A Path for Every Seeker

Gurudev's vision is profoundly inclusive—whether one is a beginner stepping into meditation for the first time, a spiritual seeker yearning for higher wisdom, or a leader seeking to bring clarity and intuition into decision-making, there is a program designed to uplift, heal, and ignite transformation at every level.

These diverse practices have touched millions across the world, serving as doorways to inner expansion, self-discovery, and lasting peace. With each breath, each moment of silence, and each meditation, the path unfolds—not as a mere technique, but as a journey into the vast, boundless realm of the Self.

Stories of Transformation: Healing, Awakening, and Renewal

The impact of Sudarshan Kriya and Gurudev Sri Sri Ravi Shankar's meditation techniques extends beyond scientific studies and statistics—it is etched in the lives of millions who have experienced profound healing, inner peace, and personal breakthroughs. From war veterans to corporate executives, from prison inmates to struggling students, the testimonials paint a vivid picture of the depth of transformation.

From Darkness to Light: Overcoming Depression and Anxiety

"For years, I struggled with severe anxiety and depression. Medication helped, but I still felt like something was missing—like I was drowning in my own thoughts. Then, I was introduced to Sudarshan Kriya. After just a few days of practice, something shifted. My mind became clearer, and I started experiencing joy for no reason. Today, I no longer rely on antidepressants, and I wake up every morning with a sense of purpose and calm."

— Lisa M., USA

Clinical studies support this transformation. Research conducted at the NIMHANS in India found that individuals practicing Sudarshan Kriya showed significant reductions in symptoms of depression and anxiety, with sustained improvements over time.

Healing PTSD: Restoring Inner Peace for War Veterans

In regions affected by war and violence, trauma runs deep in the minds and bodies of people. Many veterans and survivors struggle with post-traumatic stress disorder (PTSD), experiencing nightmares, emotional numbness, and overwhelming fear. Such techniques have remarkable therapeutic value.

"I was a soldier deployed in Iraq. The things I saw and experienced left me broken. I couldn't sleep without nightmares, and I would wake up drenched in sweat. Nothing seemed to help—until I learned Sudarshan Kriya. After just a few weeks of practice, I could sleep peacefully. The anxiety attacks stopped, and for the first time in years, I felt like myself again."

— John D., U.S. Army Veteran

Similar success stories have emerged from war-torn countries such as Iraq, Syria, and Kosovo, where Gurudev's trauma-relief workshops have helped thousands reclaim their lives.

Breaking Free: From Prison Cells to Inner Liberation

Inmates around the world, from India to South America, have experienced remarkable shifts through the Prison SMART (Stress Management and Rehabilitation Training) program, which integrates Sudarshan Kriya and meditation.

"I was sentenced to life in prison, full of regret and anger. I couldn't forgive myself for my past. When I joined the meditation program, something changed. After doing Sudarshan Kriya for the first time, I felt a deep release. I cried like never before—tears of relief. I realized that I was free, even within these prison walls."

— Carlos M., Brazil

Prison officials have reported reduced violence, increased emotional stability among inmates, and higher rates of rehabilitation among those who participate in the program.

Revitalizing Corporate Leaders: Stress Management in the Boardroom

From Fortune 500 executives to startup entrepreneurs, many have turned to Gurudev's programs to navigate stress and enhance leadership.

"I used to believe that working 16 hours a day with constant pressure was the only way to succeed. But it left me drained, irritable, and disconnected from my family. After learning Sahaj Samadhi Meditation, I found a new way to work—one that brings clarity, energy, and balance. I make better decisions, my team responds better to me, and I finally feel at peace."

— Anil R., CEO, India

Leading global corporations, including Google, Accenture, and IBM, have incorporated these practices into their employee well-being programs, seeing tangible benefits in workplace productivity and mental resilience.

Spiritual Awakening: The Journey Beyond Mind

Many seekers who attended advanced meditation retreats such as *Vigyan Bhairav* and *Sanyam* have shared experiences of profound inner silence and transcendence.

"During the Sanyam program, I experienced something beyond words. My mind became completely still, and I felt an indescribable presence—like merging with the vastness of existence. Ever since, I see life in a different way. There's an unshakable peace inside me."

— Emma L., UK

A Global Movement of Transformation

From refugee camps in Africa to bustling cities in Europe, from indigenous communities in Latin America to remote Himalayan villages, Gurudev's techniques have touched lives in every corner of the world. Whether it is Sudarshan Kriya or Sahaj Samadhi meditation, Vigyan Bhairav or Sanyam, these practices transcend boundaries of culture and religion, offering a universal path to peace and well-being.

The stories continue—each one a testament to the boundless impact of these powerful techniques. As we explore the science, the wisdom, and the experiences behind them, one truth becomes clear: Gurudev has not just taught meditation; he has reignited the spark of inner transformation for millions.

Breath is a Blessing

What is the very first act upon being born? No rocket science here, we inhale! And our very last act is to exhale. All masters have at length deliberated on the subject. Yet we need to develop the habit of being mindful of our breathing patterns and style.

From our first breath onward, every minute of our lives, we continue to breathe, taking this miraculous ability for granted because our body's autonomous system does the job so masterfully—and yet, we can control the breath and in doing so change our state of being.

We tend to think that only food provides us with the energy to survive. This is an incorrect assumption. Essentially, there are four sources of energy that sustain us. These are food, breath, rest, and a calm and meditative state of mind. The quantity of food partaken is also very significant.

As per Ayurveda there are three compartments in the stomach. One-third is meant for food, one-third for air and one-third for liquids. If we cup our palms together, it gives us an idea of the quantity of food we need to consume. Prior to every meal, a glance at cupped palms might remind us to be mindful of what we consume. We have neglected this essential aspect of life.

There are innumerable benefits to be had by practicing conscious breathing or observing the breath, not necessarily control it.

1. Physically, we can be aware as to how our breathing pattern provides oxygen to our organs. To stimulate the body's relaxation response, we need to focus on long, deep Ujjayi breaths. In this technique, practitioners should experience a sensation in the throat region. Ujjayi breaths help in elongating the breath, making it fine, smooth, and also helps in the practice of yoga. Each yogic posture we undertake can be held for a longer duration to reap maximal benefit.

In fact, we barely use thirty percent of our lung capacity. Through mindful breathing, we can also expel ninety percent of toxins.

There are several online classes being conducted by the faculty of the Art of Living under the tutelage of Gurudev Sri Sri Ravi Shankar from which individuals can learn and appreciate the magical, therapeutic prowess of pranayama.

We can undertake pain management through proper breathing exercises. If a certain part of the body is aching, one can draw all the attention to that part and observe the breath. This coupled with Mudra Pranayama works as a tonic in mitigation of pain.

2. The human mind keeps oscillating between the past and the future, never remaining in the present. Willy-nilly, this results in emotional upheaval in our system.

The mind can be brought to the present moment through the unfailing practice of the rhythmic breathing technique of Sudarshan Kriya. Gurudev Sri Sri Ravi Shankar says, "Mind is like a kite and the breath is like a string." This string can be effectively used to calm the mind through mindful breathing.

3. We can practice meditation by beginning with *Nadi Shodana (alternate nostril breathing)* pranayama. This relaxes the body, muscles, and nerves and we seamlessly slip into meditation. Meditation is an act of deconcentration where we strive to embrace all thoughts, never resisting any thought or emotion. The reality in life is that whatever we resist actually persists. Meditation eventually leads to mental sharpness and clarity and increases levels of concentration.

4. Human minds are cannonaded by innumerable thoughts. This leads to a state of perennial mental chatter. For a moment let us draw our attention to animals chewing cud, the process of regurgitation. This is exactly how we humans keep feeding on our negative thoughts and fears, re-living them every moment.

Through mindful breathing we can arrest this tendency and reduce the mental chatter, bringing our minds to the present moment. Profound silence dawns on us through mindful breathing and over a period of time antipathetic thoughts and fears in the mind dissolve, as we learn to be in the present moment, connecting to our inner self; living in harmony with our environment and our existence.

Spiritually, conscious breathing helps to remind us that energy is constantly moving. As Einstein famously said, "Nothing happens until something moves." Well, since energy is always in motion (vibration), then change is a constant in our lives! This is a truth which cannot be ignored.

Power of Pranayama

Need for pranayama

The word pranayama can be broadly divided into two segments. Prana implies the vital source of energy (the subtle life force) and *yama* is the control or extension or expansion. Therefore, pranayama can be understood as the extension of this dimension of prana.

When our energy/prana or chi levels are low, we feel enervated. This invariably occurs when we eat in gargantuan proportions rather than partake of smaller more suitable quantities, either sleep excessively or do not have adequate rest. In all such cases there is a significant expenditure of the vital life force. In these testing times, replenishing doses of energy is paramount.

Energy can be restocked through the regular practice of pranayama, yoga, and meditation. This fortifies the flow of prana through the *nadis* or energy channels in the human body to support our immune system.

Depletion of energy takes place on account of disruption in our life style, dietary indiscretions, emotional upheavals, or lack of physical exercise besides the human mind undergoing unnecessary stress. By nature, humans who do not live in the present moment latch on to the coattails of antipathetic thoughts.

Negligence on our part leads to excessive pressure on the body and mind and thereby the immune system of the body is enfeebled.

When the human mind is not in the present moment it oscillates like a pendulum between the past and the future and invariably feels distressed and distraught. Consequently, our breathing pattern becomes rapid and shallow.

Proper breathing acts like a tonic in manifold ways. It strengthens the immunity system, recharges our depleted batteries, and assuages an overwrought mind and helps to live in the present moment.

Thus, there is a deep and subtle connection between the breath, body, and mind. Effective and rhythmic breathing ensures that we live in the present, thus the mind is calm, collected, and in a meditative state. In such a state, positive endorphins are released and the body is healthy and robust to be able to combat disease.

Now through regular practice of pranayama and breathing techniques like the Sudarshan Kriya, the mind gets entrenched in the present moment. The human body is powered by five primordial elements. These are earth, water, fire, air, and space. These are all extremely important, interwoven and interrelated but it is *vayu* (air) that sustains our life. We can be without food or water for a few days but cannot survive without breathing.

Our ancient Rishis have succinctly opined that pranayama is nothing but the worship of *Vayu Devata* or the Wind God. The powers of *vayu* are immense and were known to our ancestors and the rishis. No wonder we pray to Lord Hanuman during our trials and tribulations. He is the closest to Narayana, nourishes and sustains us and strengthens our bodies physically and mentally.

Reflection & Exercises:

- Observe your breath and mental patterns before and after your practice of the Sudarshan Kriya.
- Notice a moment today when awareness shifted your mood or decision.

Personal Journal Page: Track your personal meditation experiences.

Chapter 9

A World Touched by Compassion

In a world often divided by conflict, inequality, and suffering, Gurudev Sri Sri Ravishankar's vision stands as a beacon of hope—one that transcends borders, ideologies, and social divisions. His approach to service is not merely about providing aid, but about empowering individuals and communities to rebuild their lives with dignity and resilience. From villages grappling with poverty to regions devastated by natural disasters, his humanitarian initiatives embody the philosophy of *seva*—selfless service infused with deep compassion.

Transforming Rural India: A Holistic Model for Development

Water Conservation and Agriculture

- Revival of dried-up rivers and water bodies in drought-prone regions.
- Training farmers in sustainable agricultural practices, leading to self-sufficiency.

Education and Women's Empowerment

- Free schools providing quality education to underprivileged children in rural areas.

- ✧ Vocational training and skill development programs for women, helping them achieve financial independence.

Healthcare Access in Remote Regions

- ✧ Mobile medical camps and free healthcare services for tribal communities.
- ✧ Holistic wellness initiatives, integrating Ayurveda and yoga for preventive healthcare.

Rebuilding Lives: Disaster Relief and Trauma Rehabilitation

Rapid Response to Natural Calamities

- ✧ Relief efforts during earthquakes, floods, and cyclones across India, Nepal, Sri Lanka, and beyond.
- ✧ Distribution of essential supplies, rebuilding homes, and providing medical aid.

Healing the Trauma of Conflict and Violence

- ✧ Post-war rehabilitation programs in Iraq, Kosovo, and Sri Lanka, offering emotional healing to victims of violence.
- ✧ Special stress-relief programs for soldiers and war survivors suffering from PTSD.

Global Impact: A Universal Message of Peace and Unity

Reconciliation Efforts in Conflict Zones

- ✧ Dialogues fostering peace between communities in Colombia, Lebanon, and Kashmir.
- ✧ De-radicalization initiatives providing an alternative path for those trapped in cycles of violence.

Prison Reform Through Meditation

- ✧ The Prison SMART program, which has transformed the lives of thousands of prison inmates worldwide.
- ✧ Reduction in prison violence and recidivism through breathwork and meditation practices.

Stories of Transformation: The Human Faces of Service

Beyond the numbers and large-scale initiatives, the true impact of Gurudev's humanitarian work lies in the lives it has touched. Whether it is a farmer regaining hope after years of drought, a refugee finding solace amidst turmoil, or an inmate discovering inner peace within prison walls, these narratives illustrate the profound effect of compassion in action.

A Farmer's Prayer Answered: Water Returns to the Land

Latur, Maharashtra, India

For years, **Shankar Rao**, a farmer in Maharashtra, watched helplessly as his once-thriving land turned barren. Erratic rainfall and severe drought had forced him into crippling debt, and thoughts of suicide often crossed his mind, like so many others in his village.

Then, a group of volunteers from Gurudev's River Rejuvenation project arrivedand worked tirelessly, desilting dried riverbeds, building check dams, and restoring the groundwater levels. Within months, water began to flow again.

"I had lost all hope, but now, my land is green again. My crops are growing, and I no longer think about ending my life. Gurudev has given me and my village a second chance." — **Shankar Rao**

This is not an isolated story. More than **40 rivers and thousands of water bodies** have been revived through similar efforts, restoring dignity and prosperity to countless farming communities.

Healing the Wounds of War: A Syrian Refugee's Story

A Refugee Camp, Lebanon

Fatima, a mother of three, fled Syria when war broke out, witnessing unimaginable horrors along the way. She arrived at a refugee camp in Lebanon, haunted by trauma, unable to sleep, and gripped by constant fear.

Then she attended a trauma-relief workshop conducted by trained volunteers of Gurudev's programs. Through Sudarshan Kriya and meditation, she began to release years of suppressed pain.

"I had forgotten what peace felt like. But after practicing the breathing techniques, I could sleep through the night for the first time in years. I feel stronger now, and I know I can take care of my children." — **Fatima**

Thousands of refugees like Fatima have found emotional

resilience through these programs, helping them rebuild their lives with newfound courage.

From Prison to Purpose: A Former Inmate's Journey

Tihar Jail, India

Convicted of violent crimes, **Ramesh** spent most of his life behind bars, filled with anger, regret, and hatred for the world. His life took an unexpected turn when he joined the Prison SMART program, where he learned Sudarshan Kriya and meditation.

"I never imagined that simply breathing could change me. But something shifted. The anger I held for years just melted away. I finally forgave myself."
— Ramesh

After his release, Ramesh became a yoga instructor, dedicating his life to rehabilitating other former inmates. His story is one of **thousands** where prisoners, once hardened by crime, have found transformation through mindfulness and breathwork.

A School for Those Who Had None: A Village Girl's Dream Realized

Jharkhand, India

As the daughter of daily wage laborers, **Meena** never imagined she would receive an education. Like many girls in rural India, she was expected to stay home, help with chores, and eventually marry young.

But Gurudev's vision of free schools for underserved children changed her fate. At the Art of Living school in her village, Meena received not just an education but also **nutrition, values-based learning, and self-confidence.**

"Now, I dream of becoming a teacher. I want to educate girls like me, so they never feel unworthy of learning." — **Meena**

With **700+ free schools and over 90,000 students,** the ripple effect of education is transforming entire communities.

Hope After Disaster: Rebuilding Lives After the Nepal Earthquake

📍 *Nepal*

The devastating **2015 Nepal earthquake** left thousands homeless, including **Kiran**, a father of two. His house was reduced to rubble, and despair loomed over his family.

Amid the chaos, volunteers from Gurudev's relief efforts arrived, offering **food, medical aid, and emotional support.** They didn't just rebuild homes; they helped heal minds.

"The earthquake destroyed everything we had, but these people came with open hearts and helped us start again. Their kindness gave us strength." — **Kiran**

With **over 100 disaster relief missions worldwide,** Gurudev's teams continue to provide hope where it is needed most.

Compassion in Action: A Movement of Love

These stories are a glimpse into the vast humanitarian efforts led by Gurudev Sri Sri Ravishankar. His vision extends beyond aid—it is about **empowering people to stand on their own feet, restoring dignity, and igniting the spirit of selfless service across the world.**

From villages to conflict zones, from slums to corporate boardrooms, his initiatives prove one thing: **when compassion**

leads, transformation follows.

Reflection & Exercises:

- Reflect on an act of service or compassion you witnessed or performed.
- Imagine contributing to someone's life without expectation of reward.

Personal Journal Page: Note your seva experience.

Part 3: The Essence of Wisdom – Teachings, Humor, and Timeless Insights

Chapter 10

Wisdom Nuggets

Wisdom Nuggets from Gurudev Sri Sri Ravishankar

In the realm of profound wisdom and timeless truths, Gurudev Sri Sri Ravishankar's words illuminate the path with clarity, simplicity, and an unmistakable depth that transcends intellectual comprehension. His teachings, often encapsulated in succinct yet transformative expressions, hold the power to shift perspectives, dissolve doubts, and awaken the heart to its innate joy and divinity.

The Essence of Love and Devotion

One of the most exquisite teachings of Gurudev stems from the Bhakti Sutras: *"True love knows no bargaining; it is pure, unconditional, and ever-flowing."* Love, as he expounds, is not an emotion that binds but a force that liberates. It is not a mere sentiment but the very fabric of existence.

In practical life, how do we embody this wisdom? In a world where love is often conditioned by expectations and reciprocity, Gurudev urges us to experience love as an unconditional offering.

He narrates, *"The moment you seek nothing from the other, love blossoms effortlessly."* The shift from seeking to giving transforms relationships, making them a source of boundless joy rather than entanglement.

The Art of Letting Go

One of the most recurring insights he shares is the profound freedom that comes with letting go. *"Drop the past. Just drop it. The moment you do, you are new again."*

Often, we carry the burden of resentment, regret, or guilt—allowing the past to define our present. But Gurudev's wisdom nudges us towards an effortless lightness. He explains, *"When you hold onto a grudge, whom does it hurt? Only you. Forgiveness is not doing a favor to someone else; it is freeing yourself."*

This principle finds direct application in workplaces, families, and friendships. A simple practice of observing one's emotions and choosing to release them rather than clutching onto them can bring immense peace. Meditation, breathwork, and Sudarshan Kriya—tools imparted by Gurudev—serve as practical mechanisms to facilitate this inner cleansing, expatriating both physical and mental toxins. The Nature of the Mind and Inner Stillness

Another wisdom nugget that strikes with its sheer simplicity is: *"Your mind is like a kite. It needs two things—string and wind. The string is awareness, and the wind is enthusiasm."*

The mind oscillates between the past and the future, often missing the precious moment that is now. He beautifully articulates, *"The moment you are aware that you are not in the present, you are back in the present!"* This insight becomes a guiding principle for those on the spiritual path. It emphasizes that self-awareness is the key to mastery over the mind.

Compassion as Strength

Gurudev often speaks of compassion not as an emotional weakness but as an unshakable strength. *"A weak person cannot truly be compassionate. Only one who is strong can afford to be kind."*

In leadership, business, and social service, this wisdom is invaluable. Often, we equate assertiveness with hardness, but Gurudev's teachings redefine strength as the ability to uplift, to see beyond flaws, and to hold space for others to grow. The greatest leaders and visionaries are those who act with courage, yet their hearts remain soft with empathy.

Joy Beyond Circumstances

Gurudev reminds us time and again: *"Happiness is not dependent on outer circumstances; it is an internal choice."* We often postpone joy—waiting for the perfect job, the right partner, the completion of a goal. But life is happening now. His words carry the gentle yet firm encouragement to embrace happiness as our natural state.

This realization transforms the way we approach challenges. Instead of resisting difficulties, we begin to dance with them, understanding that life is a play, and we are but actors on its grand stage. *"You have come to this world to celebrate, not to suffer."*

The wisdom of Gurudev Sri Sri Ravishankar is not merely to be admired but to be lived. Each of these teachings, when internalized and applied, has the potential to elevate life from mundane existence to a sacred celebration. Whether through love, forgiveness, awareness, compassion, or joy, his words serve as guiding stars, reminding us of our highest possibility—the limitless, blissful, and radiant self.

As Gurudev often says, *"Knowledge is not just in words; it is in being."* May we not only read these words but imbibe their essence in every breath, every thought, and every action.

Reflection & Exercises:

- Pick one teaching of Gurudev and apply it for a week. Which teaching resonates most with you, and why?

Personal Journal Page: Note down personal insights on the selected wisdom.

Chapter 11

Poetry of the Heart

Poetry flows effortlessly from a heart soaked in love and wisdom. Gurudev Sri Sri Ravi Shankar's verses are not mere words; they are echoes of the infinite, whispering the secrets of existence. His poems capture the beauty of nature, the depth of human emotions, and the transcendence of the soul's journey. They are reflections of his profound connection to the Divine—sometimes playful, sometimes piercing, but always uplifting.

Through his poetry, Gurudev takes us beyond the mundane, inviting us to experience life as a celebration, love as our very nature, and wisdom as the bridge between the known and the unknowable. Each verse carries a rhythm of stillness and a melody of awakening, dissolving boundaries between the self and the infinite. As you immerse yourself in these poems, let them not just be read, but felt—allowing their essence to unfold within you, like a silent meditation.

Just Be

"True joy is going beyond your identity,

Real rest is going beyond your desires,

Mature love is feeling the oneness,

Relax… and Just Be!

Events are transitory,

*Pick up the wisdom and be free!"**

This poem emphasizes the essence of transcending personal identities and desires to experience true joy and rest. By recognizing the transient nature of events and embracing the wisdom they offer, one can attain freedom and inner peace. The call to "Just Be" invites a state of presence and acceptance, fostering mature love through a sense of oneness with all.

You Never Know

**"You never know*

How and when

The existence will start

Using you for its purpose

You never know

How and when

You will be filled with abundance

And you will start raining

Quenching the thirst of many

You never know

How and when

You will be full of

Fruits and shade
And travelers will take
Shelter and food from you

You never know
How and when
You will be full with
Love and light
And you will start spreading
The fragrance of beauty to everyone

You never know
How and when
The death will come
And make you deathless
And life will start
Flowing out of you

You never know
*How and when... Really!"**

This poem reflects on the unpredictability of life's journey and the mysterious ways in which the Divine orchestrates our paths. It emphasizes surrendering to the flow of existence, trusting that a higher purpose unfolds through us, often beyond our immediate understanding. The verses inspire openness to transformation and readiness to serve a greater good.

I Promise

**"If I had to promise you something, what would it be?*

I can't promise that you would always be comfortable, because comfort brings boredom and discomfort.

I can't promise that all your desires will be fulfilled, because desires whether fulfilled or unfulfilled bring frustration.

I can't promise that there will always be good times, because it is the tough times that make us appreciate joy.

I can't promise that we will be rich or famous or powerful, because they can all be pathways to misery.

I can't promise that we will always be together, because it is separation that makes togetherness so wonderful.

Yet if you are willing to walk with me, If you are willing to value love over everything else.

I promise that this will be the richest and fulfilling life possible, I promise your life will be an eternal celebration, I promise you I will cherish you more than a king cherishes his crown, And I shall love you more than a mother loves her newborn.

If you are willing to walk into my arms, If you are willing to live in my heart, you will find the one you have waited forever. You will meet yourself in my arms.

*I promise."**

In this heartfelt poem, Gurudev offers a realistic perspective on life's experiences, acknowledging that challenges and discomforts are integral to personal growth. He emphasizes the transient nature of desires and external achievements, suggesting that true fulfillment arises from valuing love and inner richness over material pursuits. The promise is of a life enriched with depth, celebration, and unconditional love, transcending superficial comforts.

In his poem, **"Oh Dear, This Creation is a Celebration of Thy Presence"**, Gurudev's verses bring in a beautiful view of eternity succinctly, that makes the entire creation a celebration - *"In the world, everything reminds us of something that is not clear, something that is beyond. A hand unseen is behind this creation, and every pair of eyes is looking towards that hand which is not seen. Wherever one looks, one is looking for that hand which is behind and unseen. You look at a flower and appreciate the flower and behind the flower, there's that beauty, that truth which could bring this beauty. If this flower does not remind you of the eternal beauty, of the eternal truth, then it has not fulfilled its purpose. So, behind every activity, pleasant, unpleasant, chaotic, harmonious, is one Divinity."*

By recognizing the sacred in the mundane, one can experience life as a joyful celebration, understanding that both pleasant and challenging moments contribute to spiritual evolution. The poem encourages a shift in perspective, seeing beyond surface appearances to the divine essence pervading all.

Reflection & Exercises:

➢ Write a short poem or reflection inspired by your own spiritual or natural experiences.

Personal Journal Page: Visualize the emotion or imagery evoked by a poem.

Chapter 12

Laughter, Lightness, and Love

The Joyful Sage: Gurudev's Humor and Light-Hearted Wisdom

Laughter and wisdom are often seen as separate paths—one light and fleeting, the other deep and profound. Yet, in the presence of Gurudev Sri Sri Ravi Shankar, these two energies merge effortlessly, revealing a truth often overlooked: wisdom need not be heavy, and joy need not be superficial. His humor is spontaneous, disarming, and profoundly insightful, transforming even the most intricate spiritual concepts into something simple and relatable.

In his *satsangs,* laughter flows as naturally as meditation. With a twinkle in his eye and a playful spirit, he responds to devotees' questions with wit and spontaneity, dissolving the rigidity of the mind. Whether delivering a mischievous remark on life's ironies or slipping in an unexpected punchline mid-discourse, Gurudev reminds us that spirituality is not an escape from joy, but an immersion in it.

His humor is not merely about words—it is the very lightness of *Being.* It is the ability to look beyond the trivial and embrace the dance of life with a smile. As he so wisely states, "Taking life too seriously is a sure way to miss its essence. After all, you will never come out of it alive!" This light-hearted wisdom makes enlightenment approachable, showing us that laughter and liberation are intricately intertwined.

In this chapter, step into the joy of his presence, where profound wisdom meets delightful playfulness. Through anecdotes from *satsangs,* witty exchanges, and timeless humor, experience how Gurudev transforms everyday moments into opportunities for insight and joy—teaching not through solemnity, but through celebration.

Gurudev Sri Sri Ravi Shankar's approach to wisdom is imbued with humor, blending profound truths with moments of levity that make his teachings both accessible and transformative. His humor is not confined to clever words; it is the expression of an inner lightness that transcends the ordinary.

He once shared, "Humor is not just words; it is the lightness of your Being. You do not have to read and repeat jokes—just being cordial and light-hearted brings out authentic humor." This profound observation emphasizes that true humor emanates from a joyful, open heart. It's not about delivering punchlines, but embodying ease and connection—inviting others to relax and embrace life's flow.

He further illuminated the power of humor in relationships with this wisdom: "Humor brings everyone together, while humiliation tears them apart." In a world often divided by misunderstandings, Gurudev reminds us that humor unites, forging bonds where judgment and negativity would otherwise create division. True humor is not merely entertaining; it is healing and unifying.

Gurudev's humor also serves as a shield against life's inevitable challenges. He often says, "Humor is the buffer that saves you from humiliation. If you have a good sense of humor, you can never be humiliated." This insight reveals that humor is not just a tool for amusement; it is a resilient force—enabling one to remain composed and dignified even in the most challenging situations. It is a reminder that the ability to laugh, especially at oneself, is a sign of strength, not weakness.

One memorable *satsang* exchange highlights Gurudev's wit and divine perspective. A devotee, curious about Gurudev's choice of transportation, remarked, "Guruji, 5000 years ago, you chose a chariot as your vehicle. Now, you have chosen an Innova." Without hesitation, Gurudev replied, "I was thinking I am sitting in your heart, but you are making me sit in an Innova. I like to sit on that *aasan* (seat) which is in everyone's heart." This playful response was not simply about modes of transportation, but a gentle reminder of the omnipresence of the Divine, showing that Gurudev's true seat is in the heart of every individual, beyond the form or mode of transport.

Through these effortless exchanges, we see how Gurudev seamlessly blends humor with profound spiritual teachings, making the complex simple and the serious joyful. His anecdotes often breathe life into the timeless wisdom of ancient scriptures, such as the humorous tales of Mulla Nasruddin, whose wit carries the deepest lessons.

In one story, Mulla Nasruddin observes a successful man and remarks to his wife, "Look at him, what a successful man he is! I wish I could have his luck!" His wife responds, "Huh?" Mulla continues, "Just see, his wife's smile is much cheaper!" In this playful exchange, Gurudev highlights that the first sign of success is an unshakeable smile. While money can buy all the riches in the world, a smile comes literally free of cost. Yet, we often use it sparingly. This story encourages us to value simple expressions of joy and connection.

Another tale features Mulla's wife confronting him: "Why only four birthday gifts this year? Last year there were five! So, you don't love me the same anymore?" Mulla responds, "I love you the same but prices have increased!" Gurudev uses this humorous exchange to illustrate that demand destroys love. In relationships, giving gifts and attention is important, but when demand creeps in, seeking proof of being loved, it can become a burden. This story serves as a reminder to appreciate love without attaching conditions.

In another anecdote, Mulla's wife angrily throws a necklace on the road and walks away. Mulla observes, "Just see, his wife's smile is much cheaper!" Gurudev points out that making your smile cheaper and anger expensive can lead to a more harmonious life. He emphasizes that the first sign of success is an unshakeable smile, suggesting that a smile is invaluable, while anger costs us dearly.

Through these stories, Gurudev imparts profound life lessons with humor and simplicity, demonstrating that wisdom need not be heavy, and joy need not be superficial. His use of Mulla Nasruddin's tales serves as a gentle reminder that spirituality is not an escape from joy but an immersion into it. In doing so, Gurudev creates an environment where learning is not burdensome, but uplifting—where wisdom is as light as laughter and as joyful as the heart itself.

A similar blend of wit and wisdom can be found in His anecdotes of Swami Vivekananda -

Once, a professor asked Swami Vivekananda, "Suppose you find a book of philosophy and some money on the street, what would you take?" Without hesitation, Swami Vivekananda replied, "I would take the money." The professor, quite pleased with himself, responded, "I would take the book of philosophy, the book of wisdom!" Swami Vivekananda smiled and remarked, "That's because you take what you don't have."

In another instance, the same professor, irritated by Swami Vivekananda's simple attire, sought to insult him at a restaurant. As Swami Vivekananda sat at the same table, the professor sneered, "A pig and a bird cannot sit together at the same table." Without missing a beat, Swami Vivekananda smiled and replied, "Indeed, I can fly away anytime!" His response was effortless, free from anger, yet carried the depth of true self-knowledge. It exemplifies how a person deeply anchored in wisdom remains unshaken by provocation, rising above pettiness with grace and humor.

Just as Swami Vivekananda transformed hostility into a lesson, so too does Gurudev Sri Sri Ravi Shankar. His humor is never at the expense of others; rather, it uplifts, awakens, and lightens the heart. He teaches not through resistance but through joyful transcendence, making the journey of wisdom an experience of delight rather than a burden of seriousness.

Reflection & Exercises:

- Reflect on a time when humor diffused tension in your life.
- How can joy and humor be incorporated into daily practice?

Personal Journal Page: Record personal anecdotes of lightness or humor.

Chapter 13

Conversations with Science

Bridging Science and Spirituality: Dialogues with Gurudev Sri Sri Ravishankar

In an era where science seeks to uncover the fundamental truths of the universe, Gurudev Sri Sri Ravishankar stands as a bridge between ancient wisdom and modern discoveries. Across continents and conferences, he has engaged in profound dialogues with some of the world's leading scientists and physicists, exploring the mysteries of consciousness, the nature of reality, and the interplay between matter and energy. These conversations often leave even the most seasoned researchers reflecting on the limitations of science and the boundless dimensions of spirituality.

This chapter presents some of the most thought-provoking exchanges between Gurudev and scientific minds—discussions that not only challenge conventional knowledge but also pave the way for a integrated and holistic understanding of existence.

Gurudev Sri Sri Ravishankar's interactions with scientists and physicists highlight a profound truth—what the seers of ancient India realized through meditation and intuition is now being rediscovered by modern science. His ability to simplify deep concepts and bring clarity to the most complex questions leaves a lasting impact on those who interact with him.

As science advances, the gap between the physical and the metaphysical continues to shrink. Perhaps the greatest realization of our time will be that spirituality and science were never separate—they have always been two sides of the same cosmic mystery.

Across cultures and civilizations, the quest to unravel the nature of reality has taken two distinct yet complementary paths—one through empirical observation and scientific inquiry, and the other through inner exploration and spiritual realization. Gurudev Sri Sri Ravishankar, with his unique ability to traverse both realms, has emerged as a catalyst for bridging these two domains.

His dialogues with leading scientists are not merely exchanges of ideas; they are deep symphonies of understanding where ancient wisdom meets the rigor of modern research. In these conversations, the rigid boundaries of disciplines dissolve, revealing a unified field of knowledge that has always existed. Whether speaking with neuroscientists about the seat of consciousness, physicists about the fabric of space-time, or biologists about the interplay of breath and life, Gurudev offers a perspective that is both timeless and transformative.

What makes these discussions remarkable is not just the synthesis of knowledge but the palpable shift in perception they evoke. Scientists who come to these dialogues expecting intellectual discourse often leave with a deeper sense of wonder—one that is not just scientific but profoundly personal. They begin to see that beyond the equations and experiments lies a dimension of knowing that cannot be merely measured but must be experienced.

Our ancient rishis, through their deep inquiry, estimated the age of the current cosmic creation to be around 10 billion years—far beyond the 15,000-year timeframe held in certain traditions. Recently, European space telescopes measured the universe's age through fossil radiation from the Big Bang. Astonishingly, their findings aligned precisely with the rishis' ancient calculations. How did they arrive at such truth, devoid of technological instruments?

Because they harnessed an often-overlooked faculty—the ability to cognize through consciousness itself.

Cognition: The Inner and Outer Journey

Neuroscientists define cognition as the intricate interplay of neural networks, yet Gurudev offers a more expansive view—one that transcends the confines of the brain. He invites us to perceive awareness not merely as a function of the mind but as an all-pervading field of existence. When questioned about memory and perception, he challenges the conventional belief that consciousness is bound to neural structures, suggesting instead that memory may reside in a subtler, universal dimension. This notion echoes the ancient concept of the Akashic records—a cosmic reservoir of all knowledge and experience.

Remarkably, many discoveries heralded by modern science were already articulated in ancient texts. The principles of motion found in the Kanad Samhita, early insights resembling gravity, atomic theory, and even concepts akin to DNA were embedded in the wisdom of the past. Yet, why do Western scientific texts command such unparalleled reverence today?

Over time, the spirit of inquiry, the scientific temper that once flourished, faded into obscurity. Several forces contributed to this decline:

- Centuries of foreign rule disrupted indigenous scientific exploration.
- Sacred knowledge, safeguarded within rigid oral traditions, remained inaccessible to the masses.

- The relentless struggles of survival—wars, famine, economic turmoil—pushed intellectual pursuits to the periphery.

And yet, through the passage of time, there were those who upheld these ancient scriptures, safeguarding their wisdom against erasure. To them, we owe our gratitude—for it is their dedication that allows us to reconnect with this timeless reservoir of knowledge today.

The Mathematical Genius of the Vedas

The concept of zero—so foundational to mathematics—finds its poetic essence in the *Isha Upanishad:*

'Purnam-Adah Purnam-Idam Purnat-Purnam-Udachyate

Purnasya Purnam-Adaya Purnam-Eva-Avashishyate"

"That is full. This is full. From fullness arises fullness. Even when fullness is removed, fullness remains."

This profound mantra encapsulated the very essence of zero—a principle where addition, subtraction, and division all yield the same infinite completeness. It is a mathematical truth wrapped in spiritual profundity.

Similarly, within the rhythmic cadence of the *Rudram,* a hidden computational precision reveals itself:

'Eka cha me, tisrash cha me..."

Odd and even numbers interlace in a precise sequence—an encoded wisdom awaiting deeper exploration, its structure mirroring the harmony of the cosmos.

Beyond these verses, Vedic scholars mastered *Avadhan,* a cognitive feat of astonishing dexterity. A *Shatavadhani* could absorb and recall 100 numbers instantaneously, in any permutation. What appears miraculous is, in reality, an attunement of consciousness—a glimpse into the boundless potential of the human mind when refined through discipline and inner alignment.

The Nature of "I-ness"

In thought-provoking dialogues with physicists, Gurudev delves into the nature of identity. *"What is the 'I' that observes thoughts and emotions?"* he inquires. Neuroscientists seek its origins in neural correlates, mapping consciousness to the brain's intricate pathways. Yet, Gurudev points to a deeper substratum—one that transcends the physical.

He draws a striking parallel with quantum physics, where the very act of observation alters the observed. *"The one who observes is beyond what is observed,"* he reflects. *"And yet, the observer itself can never be fully grasped."*

This insight harmonizes with Vedantic wisdom, which proclaims that the true self is neither bound by material constructs nor defined by fleeting mental states. Instead, it is the silent witness—limitless, unchanging, and ever-present.

The Illusion of Matter

Modern science contends that matter, in its truest essence, does not exist—what we perceive as solid is merely vibration. But then, what of God? Is God a being, a force, or simply a vibration? Perhaps only vibration itself .

Asti, Bhati, Preeti—Existence, Light, and Love. Love itself is not a substance but a vibration, an unseen resonance that pervades all of creation. The world, in its multiplicity, is but *Nama* (name) and *Roopa* (form), an interplay of perception.

We sense solidity when we touch an object, yet science reveals that at the subatomic level, there is nothing but space and energy in motion. From which plane of consciousness do we truly experience reality?

Quantum mechanics has shattered classical notions of matter, showing that what appears tangible is largely empty space, held together by energetic forces. Gurudev takes this understanding deeper: *"If all is just vibration, then what is truly real?"* Physicists concede that at the quantum level, particles blink in and out of existence, defying the notion of permanence.

In these contemplations, Gurudev illuminates a profound truth—what we call 'reality' is but a projection of consciousness, a grand illusion appearing as matter. He echoes the wisdom of the *Upanishads: "The world is Maya, a fleeting mirage of the infinite."*

The Paradox of Chaos and Order

Nature bends toward entropy—disorder steadily increases over time. Yet, for life to emerge, order must prevail. How, then, did life arise from chaos?

Order and chaos are not opposing forces; they are two sides of the same cosmic rhythm. In creation, entropy escalates, culminating in dissolution. Even destruction is not an anomaly but an essential movement in the cycle of existence. Yet, in the phase of preservation, equilibrium is restored—a fleeting state of zero entropy.

Consciousness vs. Matter: What Came First?

Does matter give rise to consciousness, or does consciousness precede matter? To seek a linear answer—one before the other—is a limitation of thought. Why not consider a spherical paradigm, where both emerge simultaneously, interwoven beyond the constraints of time?

A coconut tree did not originate solely in Kerala or Hawaii. The seed of creation is not confined to a singular origin—it manifests everywhere, all at once.

Ancient Scriptures and Modern Discoveries

The *Nasadiya Sukta* of the *Rigveda*—the Hymn of Creation—speaks of an unfathomable void before existence:

"Tama Asit Tamasa Gulham..."—"Darkness was enveloped by darkness."

Neither existence nor non-existence could be defined. Within this profound verse lies the very essence of dark matter and dark energy—concepts that modern science still struggles to grasp.

Yet, a chasm remains: those deeply immersed in ancient scriptures often lack scientific training, while scientists rarely explore the vast wisdom encoded in these timeless texts. This gap must be bridged.

Gurudev does not merely discuss science—he transcends it. He invites us beyond intellectual inquiry into a direct experience of reality, where the mysteries of the cosmos and the depths of our own being are not separate frontiers, but reflections of the same boundless truth.

The Quantum Connection: Consciousness and the Observer Effect

One of the most fascinating intersections between spirituality and physics lies in quantum mechanics. In a discussion with a renowned quantum physicist, Gurudev was asked about the role of the observer in shaping reality. He smiled and responded:

"In the ancient texts, the rishis said, 'Drashta he jagat ka nirmata hai'—the seer is the creator of the world. What you observe changes with the quality of your mind. Your consciousness influences what you perceive, and what you perceive shapes your reality."

The physicist, who had spent decades studying the observer effect, was stunned. "This is precisely what quantum mechanics tells us!" he exclaimed.

Through this dialogue, Gurudev elucidated how spiritual traditions have long recognized what quantum physics is only now beginning to understand: that the act of observation is not passive but participatory in the unfolding of reality.

Beyond the Brain: The Science of Consciousness

At an international neuroscience conference, a group of scientists debated whether consciousness was merely a byproduct of brain activity or something beyond. Gurudev listened attentively and then posed a simple yet profound question:

"Can you perceive the perceiver? If consciousness is merely brain activity, then who is aware of it?"

This question sparked an intense discussion. Many agreed that despite extensive research, science has yet to explain who experiences thoughts, emotions, and existence itself. Gurudev elaborated on how ancient wisdom views consciousness not as a product of the brain, but as the fundamental essence of existence—one that pervades all of creation.

One neuroscientist later admitted, "I came here expecting to explain the brain to Gurudev, but he made me rethink everything I assumed about consciousness."

The Universe as Vibration: Sound, Energy, and the Nature of Reality

In a dialogue with astrophysicists exploring the mysteries of dark matter and dark energy, Gurudev illuminated a profound intersection between modern physics and ancient wisdom.

"Everything is vibration. The entire cosmos is but waves in constant interplay," he remarked. *"The Vedas declare—Nada Brahma—the*

universe is sound. Different frequencies of vibration give rise to different forms."

A scientist responded with excitement, *"That aligns perfectly with the String Theory! At the most fundamental level, reality is composed of vibrating strings of energy."*

Gurudev continued, *"Every mantra carries a distinct vibration, attuning the mind and body to a higher frequency. Just as varying wavelengths of light produce different colors, the subtle vibrations of sound shape consciousness in profound ways."*

The conversation left the scientists deeply intrigued, opening a doorway to the possibility that ancient practices like chanting and meditation might hold scientific truths yet to be fully understood.

The Science of Breath: Sudarshan Kriya and Well-Being

Gurudev has often spoken about the power of breath, and modern research is catching up. At a wellness summit, he was asked about the scientific basis of Sudarshan Kriya, to which he responded:

"Every emotion has a corresponding rhythm of breath. By changing the breath, you can change your emotional and mental state."

This statement is now being validated through research in neurophysiology. Studies on Sudarshan Kriya have shown that it significantly reduces cortisol levels, improves autonomic nervous system function, and even impacts gene expression. Neuroscientists attending the talk were fascinated by how an ancient practice was demonstrating tangible physiological benefits.

One researcher remarked, "We usually study meditation after it is already practiced for years. But here is someone who knows how it works first, and now we are discovering the science behind it."

Conversations with ISRO Scientists: The Cosmos and Consciousness

During a special session with scientists at the Indian Space Research Organization (ISRO), Gurudev engaged in a profound discussion on space, time, and consciousness. As the scientists explained their missions to explore the vast universe, he posed a question that shifted their perspective:

"You are searching for life in the cosmos, but have you explored the infinite space within?"

He elaborated on how the mind, like space, is infinite and uncharted. "Just as there are black holes in space that absorb light, there are states of consciousness where the mind withdraws from the external world and merges into stillness. Science has explored outer space extensively, but inner space is just as vast and mysterious."

One ISRO scientist asked about time dilation and relativity, drawing parallels with Einstein's theories. Gurudev responded,

"Time is relative not just in physics but also in experience. When you meditate, time expands. A few minutes can feel like hours, and sometimes hours pass in what feels like minutes. Ancient rishis understood this relativity long before modern science formulated equations for it."

The discussion illuminated parallels between modern space exploration and the ancient seers' inward journeys. Several remarked that this was one of the most intellectually and spiritually stimulating discussions they had ever engaged in.

The Future of Science and Spirituality

In various forums, Gurudev has emphasized the need for an integrated approach where science and spirituality complement each other.

"Science tells us how things happen, spirituality tells us why. Science measures the outer world, spirituality explores the inner world. Together, they can give us a complete picture of reality."

He has inspired many scientists to explore consciousness not just as an academic subject, but as a lived experience. His dialogues continue to shape new paradigms of research, urging scientists to look beyond materialistic frameworks and embrace a holistic view of existence.

These dialogues unveil a profound synthesis: science and spirituality are not opposing realms but complementary lenses through which we seek to understand reality. While neuroscience maps cognition and physics deconstructs matter, Gurudev offers an experiential wisdom that transcends intellectual inquiry—a direct perception of existence beyond the confines of thought.

His dialogues ignite a holistic vision where breath, consciousness, and existence are not fragmented but seamlessly intertwined. As scientists probe deeper into the mysteries of consciousness, Gurudev's insights beckon us beyond analysis—to immerse ourselves in the vast, unbounded awareness that is the very fabric of existence - an invitation to experience the profound essence of love, compassion, and Truth!

Reflection & Exercises:

➢ Explore a personal question on consciousness or science-spirituality integration.

➢ How would you integrate logic and intuition in your decision-making?

Personal Journal Page: Note the reflections on science and spirituality dialogues.

Part 4: A Life Lived in Harmony – Connection to Nature, Music, and Celebration

Chapter 14

Music as Meditation

Gurudev's Love for Music

Gurudev Sri Sri Ravi Shankar's love for music is intrinsic and profound, flowing effortlessly into his being like the gentle strains of a veena. Often, he immerses himself in its ethereal vibrations, not merely as a musician but as a seeker, attuned to the deeper resonance of sound as a bridge to silence. Under his guidance, countless musicians and artists have transcended the realm of technique to explore music as a sacred journey—one that moves beyond notes and rhythms to evoke the stillness of the soul.

For Gurudev, music is not merely an art form; it is a sacred communion with the Divine. He expresses:

"Music is that which brings harmony to life. It is not just in the notes; it is in your being."

His *satsangs* stand as luminous testaments to this wisdom, where sacred chants and soul-stirring bhajans weave an atmosphere of deep meditation and unbridled joy. Whether playing the veena, guiding a chorus of voices in a *satsang,* or simply losing himself in the spontaneous melody of a flute, his presence infuses music with an unmistakable spiritual essence. He often speaks of sound as a vehicle for inner transformation, capable of dissolving mental agitation, elevating consciousness, and leading the mind effortlessly into meditation.

As he so beautifully articulates:

"Music is that which takes you beyond music, into silence."

Through music, Gurudev unveils the secret to effortless meditation—where the heart is enraptured, the mind surrenders, and in the embrace of melody, one discovers the infinite stillness within.

Music as a Gateway to Meditation

Meditation is often envisioned as a practice of silence, yet music serves as a profound bridge, gently ushering the mind into stillness. As Gurudev Sri Sri Ravi Shankar beautifully expresses:

"When your mind is immersed in music, it is close to meditation. And when you go deep into meditation, the whole universe becomes music."

In his teachings, music is not merely an arrangement of notes—it is a pathway to transcendence. Many of his guided meditations seamlessly weave in music, allowing the mind to soften, the heart to open, and awareness to turn inward. He explains:

"When you deeply listen to music, your thoughts fade, and you enter a space of stillness. That is meditation."

Bhajans and kirtans, the soul of The Art of Living's spiritual gatherings, amplify this experience. When voices rise together in devotion, the energy transcends melody and meaning, dissolving boundaries between singer and song, sound and silence. In this sacred communion, music ceases to be an external experience and becomes an inner transformation—one that elevates consciousness and leads effortlessly into meditation.

Gurudev often reminds us that music is the language of the heart, a force that speaks beyond words and intellect. As he so eloquently says:

"Music is the language of the heart. When words fail to express, music takes over."

Through music, the restless mind finds repose, the agitated heart discovers serenity, and the entire being moves into harmony—revealing meditation in its most effortless and natural form.

From the rhythmic beats of a drum to the delicate notes of a flute, music has a way of bypassing the intellect and touching the soul. According to Gurudev, different ragas and melodies influence various emotions, and understanding this can help individuals use music as a tool for inner transformation. For instance, certain ragas bring about serenity, while others inspire joy, devotion, or even a sense of surrender.

Satsang: Elevating the Spirit Through Music

One of the most profound ways music facilitates meditation is through the practice of *satsang.* Derived from Sanskrit, *satsang* means 'the company of truth' and involves collective singing and chanting.

Gurudev often explains that in *satsang,* the combination of rhythmic clapping, chanting, and uplifting melodies creates an atmosphere of spiritual elevation. He says, *"Satsang is like a shower for the mind—cleansing, rejuvenating, and uplifting."*

Singing in a group setting is particularly powerful because it dissolves the ego, aligns individuals with higher vibrations, and makes meditation effortless. The resonance of devotional music, when sung with feeling, takes the listener beyond words and thoughts into pure experience. As Gurudev beautifully puts it, *"When you sing, your breath flows in rhythm, and that rhythm aligns with nature's rhythm. Then meditation just happens."*

Music and Chakras: Harmonizing Inner Energy

The relationship between music and the body's energy centers, or *chakras,* is another integral aspect of meditative practice. Each chakra resonates with specific musical notes and sounds, and engaging with these frequencies can activate and balance the energy flow within the body. Gurudev explains that music, when aligned with certain vibrations, can open blockages in the subtle energy system and restore harmony.

For instance, the *Muladhara* (root) chakra, located at the base of the spine, responds to deep and grounding sounds, while the *Anahata* (heart) chakra resonates with uplifting melodies that evoke love and compassion. The *Ajna* (third eye) chakra, associated with intuition and wisdom, can be stimulated through subtle, high-frequency sounds such as those produced by certain mantras and flute compositions. Gurudev often advises meditators to listen to music that resonates with their inner state and assists them in aligning with nature's rhythm.

The Universal Language of Music

Gurudev Sri Sri Ravi Shankar often speaks about how music transcends language, culture, and boundaries, making it a universal tool for healing and connection. He shares how music has been a part of spiritual traditions across civilizations—from Vedic chants in India to Sufi music in Persia, from Gregorian chants in Europe to African tribal rhythms. He says, "No matter where you are from, music touches the same emotions in every heart. It is the simplest way to unite people and uplift humanity."

Whether through the collective joy of *satsang,* the deep resonance of *ragas,* or the subtle harmonization of *chakras,* music as meditation offers a transformative journey toward inner tranquility and spiritual enlightenment.

The Grand Musical Feats of the Art of Living Foundation

Under Gurudev's leadership, the Art of Living Foundation has pioneered global musical events that showcase the unifying and meditative power of music. Some of the most remarkable feats include:

✧ **Antarnaad (2009):** A historic symphony of 2,750 Indian classical vocalists coming together in Pune to create a mesmerizing spiritual experience.

✧ **Naad Vaibhav (2012):** A grand event in Bengaluru where thousands of musicians played ancient ragas, invoking deep serenity and devotion.

✧ **World Culture Festival (2016):** A breathtaking musical spectacle where 8,500 musicians performed on one stage, celebrating unity in diversity through music.

✧ **Sahasra Veena Jhenkara (2022):** An ensemble of 1,116 veena artists performing in unison, demonstrating the divine essence of classical Indian music.

These events are not just performances but mass meditative experiences, where music becomes a conduit for inner stillness, connecting thousands of people in collective harmony.

Music, in Gurudev's vision, is a journey from sound to silence, from activity to stillness, and from chaos to bliss. Whether through grand symphonies or the simple strumming of a single instrument, it has the power to transport individuals to a meditative state. In this way, music becomes not just an experience but a profound spiritual practice that leads one to the depths of the self.

Reflection & Exercises:

- Practice mindful listening to music today and note emotional shifts.
- Which sound or rhythm brings you the most peace?

Personal Journal Page: Rrecord your meditation experiences through music.

Chapter 15

Dance with Nature

There is a rhythm in nature, a silent music that plays through the rustling of leaves, the chirping of birds, the flow of rivers, and even the gentle touch of the breeze. For most, nature is something to be admired from a distance, but for Gurudev Sri Sri Ravi Shankar, it is an intimate companion—a reflection of the Divine, a dance of existence in which every being, and every element, has its own unique step.

Wherever he goes, nature seems to respond to him—not just in the poetic sense, but quite literally. Birds gather around him, animals approach him with an inexplicable trust, and even the elements themselves seem to conspire to create an aura of magic. It is as though he carries within him a harmony that the natural world instantly recognizes.

He often says, *"When you are with nature, you start singing, you communicate with nature from your heart. Nature is not outside of you. You are nature. When you realize this, a deep sense of belonging dawns, and with it, a profound joy."*

Let us step into this delightful journey and witness how he dances with nature.

The Playfulness of Snow

In the serene whiteness of snow-covered landscapes, one would expect a spiritual master to remain in quiet contemplation. But Gurudev surprises everyone—his childlike playfulness knows no bounds. He marvels at the snowflakes, catching them in his hands, watching them dissolve like fleeting moments of life. He does not just walk through the snow; he embraces it, feeling its softness, its silence, and the way it transforms the world into a canvas of purity.

Once, during a trip to the mountains, a group of devotees watched in amusement as Gurudev picked up a handful of snow and playfully tossed it at them. A spontaneous snowball fight ensued, laughter filling the crisp mountain air. "It is important to play," he said with a smile. "Playfulness is the nature of the spirit. When you forget to play, you forget to live."

Even in moments of sheer joy, there was always a deeper wisdom. Standing in the middle of the snow, he reflected, *"Life is like a snowflake—beautiful, delicate, and ever-changing. You cannot hold on to it, but you can marvel at its beauty while it lasts."*

The Language of the Birds

Birds seem to recognize Gurudev's presence even before people do. It is a common sight—wherever he sits in silence, birds gather, chirping, cooing, singing, as if engaging in a lively conversation with him. Peacocks dance in his presence, their iridescent feathers shimmering in the sunlight, responding to an unspoken rhythm.

He once shared a beautiful insight: *"Birds sing not for an audience, but because it is their nature to sing. When you live your life like that, without seeking approval or appreciation, you become free."*

A devotee once asked why birds and animals seemed so drawn to him. He smiled and said, "They don't see the masks that humans do. They recognize only vibrations. When your mind is still and heart is pure, nature trusts you completely."

The Gentle Giants: Indrani & Maheshwara

Elephants are often associated with wisdom, memory, and strength, but in Gurudev's presence, they become playful children. Indrani and Maheshwara, two majestic elephants at the Art of Living ashram, greet him with boundless affection. Their large trunks nuzzle him gently, their eyes reflecting a deep sense of connection.

On one occasion, as he approached Indrani, she trumpeted with joy and wrapped her trunk around him as if embracing an old friend. Maheshwara, known for his strength, softened instantly, lowering his head in reverence.

"Even the mightiest bow down in love," Gurudev mused. "True strength is not in domination but in gentleness."

He often reminds us that nature operates from a space of love and trust: *"When you meet the world with love, even the strongest creatures will respond with gentleness."*

Whispers with the Wind

There is something poetic about the way Gurudev stands amidst nature, feeling the wind brush against his face, his eyes closed as if listening to a language only he can hear. The wind, he says, carries messages from the past, whispers from the ancients, and the laughter of the Divine.

On a particularly breezy evening, standing under a massive banyan tree, he shared: *"The wind does not struggle; it moves effortlessly. When you move like the wind, unattached yet present, you become free."*

At times, the wind would pick up just as Gurudev spoke of something profound, as if the universe itself nodded in agreement. Those who have been in his presence during such moments have often felt as if nature conspires to magnify his words.

Riding with Grace: The Language of Horses

Gurudev's connection with horses is something extraordinary. Unlike most riders who control a horse with reins, he communicates with them through presence alone. He often says, "A horse does not obey force; it responds to trust."

Once, while riding through the lush greenery of the ashram, his horse suddenly stopped. Instead of urging it forward, Gurudev simply placed a hand on its neck and whispered something. Almost immediately, the horse resumed its pace, moving in perfect rhythm with him.

A devotee watching this scene asked, "What did you tell the horse?" Gurudev smiled and said, "I just told him that we are one."

His ability to move in harmony with animals reflects his deep realization that separation is an illusion. *"In oneness, there is no need for command—only understanding."*

Sacred Waters and Stillness

Sitting by a river, Gurudev once watched as the ripples spread across the water's surface. He picked up a small stone, dropped it gently, and observed the concentric circles expand outward.

"This is how every thought affects the universe," he said. "Every action, every word, creates ripples. But see—the river does not hold on to them. It flows, allowing them to dissolve. That is meditation."

For him, rivers are not just bodies of water; they are symbols of surrender, resilience, and wisdom. *"Be like a river," he often says. "Flow through life with grace, nourishing everything in your path, yet remaining unattached."*

The Grand Dance of Life

Every tree, every wave, every rustling leaf is a part of a grand cosmic dance, and Gurudev moves through this dance with effortless grace. His connection to nature is not a mere appreciation but a profound realization that there is no separation.

In his own words: *"The whole universe is a play of consciousness. The waves dance in the ocean, the wind dances in the sky, and life itself is a celebration. When you recognize this, you, too, become the dance."*

This chapter, much like nature itself, is a celebration of harmony, joy, and the unspoken bond among all living beings. Through Gurudev's eyes, we see that nature is not something to be conquered or controlled—it is to be embraced, revered, and ultimately, danced with.

Reflection & Exercises:

- Spend time outdoors and observe nature mindfully.
- How does nature reveal interconnectedness in your life?

Personal Journal Page: Note your personal experiences of being in nature.

Chapter 16

Festivals of Joy

The Celebration of Festivals with Gurudev Sri Sri Ravi Shankar

Festivals are not merely dates inscribed on the calendar; they are expressions of joy, devotion, and deep spiritual wisdom. Across cultures, celebrations bring people together, reminding them of the deeper significance of life—gratitude, renewal, devotion, and unity. Under the radiant presence of Gurudev Sri Sri Ravi Shankar, every festival transforms into a grand celebration infused with spiritual depth, vibrant joy, and a universal message of oneness.

At the Art of Living International Center, nestled amidst the serene hills of Bangalore, festivals from every corner of India and the world find a home. Whether it is the intensity of Mahashivratri, the reverence of Navratri, the colors of Holi, or the radiance of Diwali, each celebration becomes a time of deep reflection, devotion, and boundless happiness. Gurudev's very presence magnifies the joy, making every moment luminous and every ritual a doorway to the divine.

He often says, "Life itself is a festival. And when you celebrate with wisdom, every moment becomes a festival."

Let us step into the splendor of these festivals, as celebrated in the presence of a living master.

Mahashivratri: A Night of Divine Awakening

One of the most awaited and spiritually powerful nights at the Art of Living International Center is Mahashivratri. Lakhs of devotees from across the globe gather at the ashram to experience the Shiva Tattva—the infinite consciousness that pervades all existence.

As the sun sets and there is a red glow in the skies, the atmosphere transforms into a sacred space of deep meditation, soul-stirring chants, Rudrabhishekam, and the powerful midnight meditation led by Gurudev.

He explains, *"Mahashivratri is not about rituals alone. It is the night of wakefulness, the night of deep rest, the night when the individual dissolves into the infinite. It is the night of the union of Shiva and Shakti, where stillness and dynamism become one."*

With each chant of "Om Namah Shivaya," one can feel a deep silence taking over, an immersion into a state beyond words. The Mahashivratri celebrations at the ashram are not just events; they are transformational experiences, where seekers from all walks of life merge into the vastness of consciousness.

Navratri: The Nine Nights of the Divine Mother

Navratri at the ashram is an extraordinary spiritual experience, welcoming devotees from all corners of the world. These nine nights are dedicated to the worship of Devi—the divine feminine energy that governs all of creation.

The celebrations begin with pujas, yajnas, and deep meditation, culminating in the grand Chandi Homa, a powerful fire ritual invoking divine blessings.

Gurudev explains, *"Navratri is a time to purify the body and mind, to go inward, and to rejoice in the grace of the Devi. Each night represents a different facet of the Divine Mother—strength, wisdom, love, and transformation."*

Every evening, devotional music, dance, and *satsangs* fill the air with a celebratory spirit. On the final night, Vijayadashami, the victory of wisdom over ignorance is celebrated with great fervor.

It is a time when one does not merely worship the Divine Mother but experiences her presence within.

The Hues of Holi: Colors of Love and Unity

Holi at the ashram is an explosion of joy, colors, and divine love. Thousands gather to celebrate, throwing vibrant hues into the air, symbolizing the letting go of past burdens and embracing life with freshness and enthusiasm.

Gurudev often joins the revelry, playfully smearing colors on devotees, reminding them, "Life is like Holi—it is meant to be colorful and joyful. When you see the world as colors of the Divine, everything becomes a celebration."

He also shares the deeper significance of Holi:

"Burn your negativity in the Holika Dahan (bonfire of Holi) and enter the next phase of your life with love, laughter, and wisdom."

As music and laughter fill the air, one realizes that Holi is more than just colors—it is about dropping all barriers, dissolving differences, and embracing the oneness of life.

Sankranti: The Simplicity of Til and Gud

Sankranti marks the Sun's transition into a new zodiac sign, signifying renewal, warmth, and the eternal movement towards light. It is a time of change, of bidding farewell to the past and embracing new beginnings. The festival is celebrated with vibrant kite-flying, glowing bonfires, and the cherished tradition of sharing til (sesame) and gud (jaggery), which carry a profound spiritual message.

Gurudev Sri Sri Ravi Shankar beautifully explains,

"Til and gud represent harmony in relationships. Jaggery is sweet, til is strong. Just like them, our relationships must have both strength and sweetness.

The simple sesame seed and jaggery offer a subtle yet profound wisdom. They remind us to cultivate inner purity. Gurudev elaborates: If you scrub the sesame seed, it turns white on the outside too. We are like a sesame seed in this vast universe—infinitesimal in the grand scheme of existence. But the moment arrogance creeps in—the thought 'I am something'—the downfall begins. This is an experiential truth. The instant one clings to power or pride, its decline is inevitable.

Just as the sesame seed holds oil within, divinity pervades this universe, residing in every heart. To recognize this is the highest wisdom, the knowledge of the Self.

Sankranti is not merely a festival—it is a reminder to move towards light, to stay humble, and to nurture both inner purity and outer sweetness in all that we do."

Diwali: The Festival of Inner and Outer Light

Diwali at the ashram is a mesmerizing spectacle of lights, devotion, and deep spiritual significance. The evening begins with a grand Lakshmi Puja, where lamps are lit to invite abundance, wisdom, and prosperity.

Gurudev shares, "Diwali is not just about lighting lamps outside; it is about lighting the lamp of wisdom within. When your inner light shines, darkness cannot touch you."

As the night unfolds, fireworks illuminate the sky, laughter echoes, and a deep sense of gratitude fills the air. The ashram radiates a glow of love, knowledge, and celebration.

Karthik Purnima: The Full Moon of Devotion

Under the luminous full moon of Karthik Purnima, devotees gather by the lake to light floating diyas, symbolizing offering their aspirations to the Divine.

Gurudev says, "Karthik Purnima is a day when divine energies are at their peak. When you light a lamp on this day, you are lighting up your inner world." Chants, bhajans, and the sacredness of the night make it a sublime experience of devotion and inner awakening.

A Celebration Beyond Religion

Festivals are more than rituals and customs; they are experiences that elevate the soul. Gurudev brings out the essence of each celebration, dissolving all differences and making it an opportunity for growth, joy, and deeper wisdom.

As he often says, "Festivals are reminders that life is a gift, to be celebrated with wisdom, devotion, and a heart full of gratitude."

To celebrate in his presence is to experience the magic of tradition, the joy of togetherness, and the depth of spirituality—all woven into one divine symphony of celebration.

Guru Purnima: The Festival of the Eternal Guiding Light

If there is one day that outshines all festivals in the heart of a seeker, it is Guru Purnima.

On this day, the full moon shines with an ethereal glow, symbolizing the illumination of wisdom in the presence of the

Guru. It is a day of profound significance, where disciples gather to express their gratitude to the eternal Guru principle—the force that dispels darkness and awakens the highest knowledge.

Gurudev often speaks of Guru Purnima not as a ritual, but as a moment of transformation:

"All celebrations in the world are for something outside of you. But Guru Purnima is a festival of the soul—it is when the disciple wakes up to the presence of the Guru within, to the light that was always there, but unseen."

The grandeur of Guru Purnima is unparalleled. The morning begins with an atmosphere charged with devotion, with thousands sitting in deep meditation, his mere presence igniting a wave of stillness. The Paduka Puja (offering to the sandals of the Guru) is performed, not as a mere custom, but as a recognition of the path that leads one from bondage to liberation.

What makes Guru Purnima unique is its depth—unlike festivals that celebrate external victories, this day celebrates the inner journey, the triumph of wisdom over ignorance. It is the day when seekers around the world pause, reflect, and renew their commitment to walk the path of truth.

Gurudev reminds, *"The Guru is not a person, but a presence. When you dissolve into that presence, the entire existence becomes a festival."*

That is why for a devotee, Guru Purnima is not just a celebration; it is life itself, woven into one moment of absolute surrender and bliss.

Gurudev's presence adds a different dimension to festivity—one that is not bound by customs alone, but flows into the realm of experience.

As he says, "Celebration is not just about external festivity. It is about awakening the joy within you, discovering the silence within the noise, the eternal within the fleeting. When the heart is full, life itself becomes a festival."

And so, in his presence, every moment sparkles, every gathering becomes sacred, and life itself turns into an eternal celebration.

In that quiet recognition, something settles—leaving behind not answers, but a deeper knowing.

Celebrations continued in form of a major event in the capital city of India which show cased various art forms. This has been a singular initiative by Gurudev Sri Sri Ravi Shankar and the Art of Living Foundation.

World Culture Festival — The Background

Gurudev Sri Sri Ravi Shankar, in his talismanic manner, is spiritually rejuvenating the country and the world. The corner stone of this modern-day spirituality are—*sadhana, seva, satsang* and smile. Gurudev is 'Making India' the spiritual capital of the world.

Well aware that happiness is the bedrock of spirituality, Gurudev always poses only one question to the seeker, "Are you happy?" Truly, he has been spreading waves of happiness across India and the globe.

Gurudev, among others, believes in reviving and showcasing our rich cultural heritage to the vast swathes of the Indian and world population. The Art of Living became the platform for both aspiring and accomplished artistes to perform, individually or in large groups, through symphonies, ensembles, and orchestras.

Devotees are well aware that to mark 25 years of its existence, The Art of Living organized the Silver Jubilee celebrations between 16 and 18 February 2006. The event, the first of its kind in several respects is fondly remembered by the followers of Gurudev Sri Sri Ravi Shankar among others for the evocative display of cultural fireworks.

The event exhibited the tapestry of Indian culture and traditions to an estimated 2.5 million people.

That was just the beginning.

Gurudev has, over the years, transcended all boundaries and we have been treated to several performances by eminent artistes and also by tyros and promising amateurs, who otherwise might have remained in the confines of anonymity. "Your ability to take risks is directly proportional to your success," says Gurudev.

One can add another S to the of Art of Living path—symphony; which together make the organization so unique.

"While witnessing a dance recital such as Kuchipudi, I would like to see a thousand hands of Durga emanating," says Gurudev Sri Sri Ravi Shankar. That should be the indelible impression created on the minds of the viewer. Or imagine 2,000 artistes playing the veena, or 2,000 artistes playing the sitar, the flute, the mridangam, pakhavaj or any other instrument, in unison. The energy levels would increase manifold and the event would become an arresting visual treat for the observer who in turn is transported to a divine stratosphere.

Gurudev has been promoting Indian classical music, dance, and our variegated traditions at several places in the country during *satsangs* and through special programs. Indian culture is now not merely confined to the traditional kutcheries and sabhas or elite auditoriums. It is denizens of the country who have been exposed to various folk and classical forms.

Only a fortunate few can view traditional and esoteric art forms in a live performance. The majority view it electronically or through the social media. WCF was one occasion when the potentate and the populace witnessed the events together in harmony.

It may be mentioned that prior to entering the sanctum *(garbha griha),* a devotee can see engravings and embellishments of various artists, dancers, and singers on the walls of our temples. This has been part of our rich cultural heritage. In that quiet recognition, something settles—leaving behind not answers, but a deeper knowing.

Those familiar with Tamil may have learnt or heard a famous rendition:

Karpagavallinin Porpadangal Pidithen

Nargathi Aruvavai Amma

Parpalarum Potrum Padimayilapuriyil

Sirpam Migunda Uyar Singara Kovil Kondu

The verse translates to: 'I seek refuge in the golden feet of Karpagavalli (Goddess Parvati), who is resident in a resplendent temple replete with finest sculpture and praised by one and all; Oh goddess! Grant me a good standing.' This verse eulogizes Karpagavalli (Goddess Parvati) of Mylapore (in Chennai).

The seven-acre stage of the World Culture Festival was a holy temple where the Gandharvas themselves seemed to have descended to perform. And seated amidst all Gandharvas was Narayana himself.

World Cultural Festival — The Details

The event commemorated 35 years of yeoman service to humanity by the Art of Living. The congregation at the WCF included peacemakers, spiritual leaders, law makers, politicians, and artists under one roof spreading the message of peace and harmony.

Around 3.5 million people gathered and celebrated the rainbow of rich cultural traditions – a pot-pouri of dance, music, arts, cuisine, yoga, and meditation.

The mammoth task of assembling more than 25,000 artists who performed in harmony to the assembled multitudes was sheer Mandrake-like magic, which could be conjured up only by Gurudev.

The atmosphere reverberated to Vedic incantations, a centuries old inaugural tradition. The chanting of hymns was followed by an ensemble of traditional Indian dance forms from Kathak, Bharatanatyam, Mohiniyattam, Kathakali and Kuchipudi to Odissi.

Different states of India showcased their rich heritage, culture, and dance forms to clockwork precision. The artistes toiled hard and put in several hours of practice to achieve perfection. They were in pursuit of excellence to enthrall the Master and followers.

The foreign complement ranged from the Horo dance of Bulgaria, African beats, Whirling Dervishes from exotic Turkiye, Awa Odori from the land of the Rising Sun, Brazilian Samba (which inspires their footballers to excel at any stage) and the Russian, Belarussian and Lithuanian dance formats.

South-east Asia was represented by the Filipino traditional dance and Mongolian and Indonesian performances. Nepal and Sri Lanka, our SAARC neighbours added spice to the exotic menu. The USA treated those assembled to high energy and eclectic Hip Hop dances.

The performances were interspersed with grand symphonies, Rabindra Sangeet, and Sufi music from Pakistan. The piece de resistance was the 'Cosmic Rhythm', a confluence of over 3000 artistes from across the globe.

High octane dance performances and mellifluous musical renditions were tempered by yoga and meditation sessions conducted by Gurudev.

Guided meditation conducted by Pujya Gurudev was indeed a cathartic experience for the devout and those assembled. One was purged of all negative thoughts and experienced pure bliss. It was like what is known as the 'Maharishi Effect.' An interfaith meet of 2,000 saints from all religions who shared the gospel truth of peace and non-violence was organized. Two thousand Vedic pandits from various Gurukuls of the country chanted in unison to promote world peace.

World Culture Festival - The Event

Delhi was soaked by rains on 11 and 12 March 2016. Naysayers predicted that the weather would be tumultuous, tempestuous, and inclement during a better part of the weekend.

Yes, the World Culture Festival of the Art of Living was planned between 11th and 13th of March. As the faithful gathered in vast multitudes the skies opened and all were soaked, drenched in the downpour that followed.

Strangely, no one fell ill despite the thunderous rain. The only individual (also thoroughly drenched as the umbrella shielding him flew off) who suffered with a terrible cold, cough, and possible fever was Pujya Gurudev.

Gurudev protected the devotees by bearing the brunt and fury of nature. Lord Krishna, too, protected the gopas and gopikas of Nand Gaon by lifting the Govardhan mountain to save them from the wrath of Indra. Who says miracles do not occur? A discerning observer has to just flow with the tide to see them unfold as was witnessed during those three days and on several other occasions.

There is a plant called Lakshmitaru. It has been making waves across the globe for certain inherent medicinal properties. A few saplings were transported from Bangalore to Delhi by Rajdhani Express as important dignitaries were to water the plants during the WCF. For certain reasons, the event did not fructify at Delhi. However, the Master remembered and conjured a little trick and saw to it that these were watered by another set of dignitaries on 19th March at the Bangalore Ashram during the veena recital (World Culture Festival culminated on that day). Gurudev has such an eye for detail, which only a Siddha Purush can possess. Thus, in the process those at Sri Sri Agricultural Trust were not disappointed. After all, to make people happy is the motto of the Art of Living.

There were a large number of artistes and devotees travelling back from Delhi to their respective destinations by different trains. Even though Parliament was in session, all the Emergency Quota tickets available by different trains (which is normally availed by VIPs and Members of Parliament) was surprisingly provided to the Art of Living family and those who had gathered to perform during the World Culture Festival. This happened so seamlessly and effortlessly that no one was left stranded. In addition, there were no reports of a VIP complaint received.

We all are blessed to be born in the times of Gurudev Sri Sri Ravi Shankar.

Those who have not learnt the unique breathing technique of Sudarshan Kriya should immediately do so and learn the knowledge of Sutras as revealed by Guruji himself. It has transformed the lives of millions of people across the globe. Why does one miss the opportunity to sport that smile and get rid of stress and anxiety.

Gurudev Sri Sri Ravi Shankar has taken birth to alleviate the pain of humanity and to bring smiles on the faces of millions of people across the globe. It would be significant to add that several Christians, while doing Sudarshan Kriya, have many a time had a glimpse of Jesus Christ.

Readers too might have the glimpse of the God or Prophet of the faith they follow.

World Culture Festival: The Fallout

The Cassandras of doubt and the prophets of doom were rendered speechless once the curtains were drawn on the World Culture Festival on the 13 March 2016.

With Pujya Gurudev's vision and guidance, the WCF 2016 saw a mesmerizing confluence of cultures from across the globe. The WCF witnessed a convergence of enthusiasm, dedication, and selfless service of Art of Living teachers, volunteers, numerous cultural teams from various states and countries.

Those who witnessed the event live or through the electronic media are indeed blessed souls. The inclement weather did not deter devotees, followers, faithful or even curious onlookers from congregating in such large numbers. It was their unabashed devotion to Gurudev and love for the Master which provided them with such determination to assemble in multitudes. People with small minds, limited vision and thinking and those inimical to the growth of the Art of Living and the phenomenal popularity of Pujya Gurudev tried their utmost to apply road blocks and put spokes in the wheels to jeopardize the event. However, their evil designs were rendered unsuccessful and the flags of 155 countries and that of Art of Living was fluttering atop the magnificent seven-acre stage triumphantly and with great majesty.

The Art of Living as envisioned by Gurudev has now been propelled into the stratosphere.

Rendition of *Mahisasur Mardini* by Chitra Roy was an extremely poignant moment in the event. As the Bhajan was sung with remarkable devotion and passion and Gurudev was slowly slipping into a trance.

This massive event was achieved with remarkable finesse and humility. This needs to be appreciated by all. Humility is the cornerstone of any meaningful success. And the organization maintained this trait faithfully. The noted industrialist and perhaps India's richest man aptly puts it, 'The aim should be to raise existing bars to unimaginable, even audacious levels — whether it is scale, quality, or something else. Don't target just growth, target exponential growth. Think big and build your very own unique and ambitious vision.'

In the ultimate analysis, this was the triumph of the big mind and superior intelligence over the petty and the small mind.

Reflection & Exercises:

➢ Identify a celebration in your life and reflect on its deeper meaning.

➢ How would you bring mindfulness and gratitude into celebrations?

Personal Journal Page: Record your personal experience at any spiritual event/festival, if you have attended one.

Part 5: Transformation and Impact – Stories of Global Change

Chapter 17

Lives Touched, Hearts Healed

Stories of Grace and Transformation Across the World

Grace does not announce itself with fanfare. Often, it arrives like a quiet wind—unbidden, unexpected, and yet unmistakable. Across continents and cultures, individuals have found themselves standing at the threshold of profound change, not through intellectual understanding alone, but through the gentle, abiding presence of a living Master. What follows are glimpses into such journeys—some marked by raw struggle, others by deep skepticism—yet all underscored by healing that resonates in body, mind, and heart.

Healing does not always arrive as an event. Often, it unfolds as a quiet shift—of breath easing, of the mind softening, of the heart finding courage to release what it has carried for long. Across cultures, geographies, and life circumstances, people have encountered Gurudev Sri Sri Ravi Shankar in ways that defy uniform description. Some speak of relief from physical suffering, others of emotional release, mental clarity, or a renewed sense of meaning.

What follows are voices from different corners of the world—each distinct, each deeply personal. These are not accounts of identical outcomes, but of individual transformations shaped by readiness, receptivity, and grace. Together, they offer glimpses into how presence itself can become a catalyst for healing—touching lives gently, yet irrevocably.

1. From Shadows of Trauma to Emotional Release

In the corridors of human experience, trauma leaves marks both seen and unseen. Some come burdened by memories they carry like hidden weights, their hearts sealed against joy. In one such story from the Sri Sri Stories archive, a seeker speaks of the unbearable grip of past pain—until, in the supportive circle of practice and presence, the walls began to soften. In moments of meditative stillness and guided breath, unarticulated grief found space to dissolve, and what had seemed permanent began to soften into peace. This was not a quick fix, but a **deep release that unfolded through inner surrender**, rippling outward into relationships and daily life.

2. Chronic Stress and Illness Finding Relief

Healing often unfolds on the body's terrain as well. Many who carried the heavy weight of chronic stress, physical infirmity, or prolonged illness have shared how the introduction of breath and meditation became more than practice— *it became a lifeline.* One individual, debilitated by paralytic syndrome and told recovery was uncertain, shared how faith, breathing practices, and surrender brought relief and restored function within days. Their narrative, contextualized within the supportive embrace of community and spiritual practice, stands as a testimony to the **confluence of inner resilience and grace** in the face of bodily challenge.

Similarly, countless others have chronicled how consistent practice of breathing techniques helped ease symptoms of depression, stress, and anxiety, gradually bringing lightness to what once felt like an unending heaviness. Such stories speak not only of symptomatic relief, but of an awakening to inner agency, allowing individuals to meet their lives with renewed strength and clarity.

3. The Skeptic Who Discovered Stillness

There are those who begin their journey with doubt—curious, perhaps, but far from certain. One such seeker entered a meditation program more out of companionable insistence than conviction, initially holding skepticism like a shield. Yet as the practices unfolded—breath by breath, moment by unfolding moment—something shifted. The habitual noise of the mind softened; the restless became still, not through effort but through a deepening sense of ease that surprised even the skeptic. This transformation was not an intellectually argued conversion, but the **soft alchemy of presence meeting resistance with patience and compassion.**

4. A Caregiver's Renewal of Resilience

Service and care for others often extracts a heavy toll from the heart of the caregiver. Yet in many stories, there emerges a beautiful reversal: those who had given so much of themselves found themselves replenished from within. In families grappling with illness, aging, or even crisis, the regular practice of breath, meditation, and mindful presence became a source of strength—not only easing the caregiver's own psychological load, but allowing them to show up with renewed equanimity and love. Such transformation ripples outward: the caregiver who once felt depleted began to approach each day with **steadiness, compassion, and inner calm,** becoming a living bridge of support rather than a reservoir of fatigue.

5. Contrasts Across Generations: The Young Seeker and the Elder Devotee

The tapestry of healing spans generations. In some accounts, a young seeker—eager, curious, sometimes restless—found in the practices a grounding that shaped his journey toward purpose and calm. In others, an elderly devotee, whose life had been textured with years of joy and sorrow alike, found in meditation and presence a renewed sense of ease and acceptance.

These generational contrasts illuminate one truth: age does not determine openness, nor does youth preclude profundity. What binds all seekers together is **the encounter with presence that whispers to the heart, beyond words, beyond expectation.**

These stories do not suggest uniformity of experience nor promise universal outcomes. Rather, they point toward a subtler phenomenon: when a seeker's readiness meets a field of compassion, healing often follows—not as a guarantee, but as a lived possibility. Whether through breath, stillness, mindful presence, or the resonance of community, individuals find in their hearts a renewal that reorients their lives toward growth, balance, and deeper awareness.

In every narrative, one finds echoes of a timeless truth: **healing is not merely the absence of suffering, but the emergence of wholeness**—an inner alignment that infuses body, mind, and spirit with renewed harmony.

Gurudev Sri Sri Ravi Shankar teaches that the secret of healing lies in accessing the body's innate intelligence through deep rest, meditation, and breathwork like Sudarshan Kriya. Healing involves releasing deep-seated stress from the cellular level, changing one's mindset (sankalpa) from sickness to wellness, and nurturing a sattvic diet and a connection with the divine.

Key aspects of healing according to Gurudev include:

✧ **The Power of Breath:** Ninety percent of toxins are released through the breath. Deep, rhythmic breathing techniques like Sudarshan Kriya directly affect the nervous system, reducing stress and initiating healing.

✧ **Deep Rest & Meditation:** True healing occurs when the mind transcends, entering a state of deep rest without inertia, often achieved through meditation.

✧ **Mindset and Determination *(Sankalpa)*:** A strong mind can carry a weak body; believing in one's ability to get better is crucial for recovery.

✧ **Dietary Habits:** Consuming fresh, nutritious food (raw honey, ginger, nuts, fruits) and avoiding stale, oily, or heavy food helps maintain a high energy level.

✧ **Consciousness as Healer:** The body is a manifestation of consciousness; aligning with this universal energy allows the cells to repair themselves.

✧ Gurudev emphasizes that the self is the ultimate healer, and by connecting with one's inner self, one can find freedom from chronic illness.

His Holiness often speaks of **healing as a natural consequence of Presence**—a quiet unfolding rather than an act of intervention. He describes this healing as a gentle progression.

Sāmīpyam—the healing that begins simply by being near.

In the proximity of a source of elevated consciousness—be it a realized teacher or a consecrated space—the restless mind begins to soften. Without effort, one starts to mirror the stillness and harmony that pervade that presence.

Sānnidhyam—the healing that deepens through felt presence.

Here, the atmosphere itself becomes transformative. The palpable field of awareness silences inner turbulence, eases anxiety, and allows the mind to rest in a state of effortless calm.

Sāyujyam—the healing of union.

In this culminating state, all sense of separation dissolves. One no longer seeks healing; one *is* whole. Misery finds no foothold where unity prevails.

This sacred movement—from being near, to feeling the presence, to becoming one—reveals healing not as a remedy, but as a remembrance. As distance dissolves, wholeness is restored, touching the spiritual, the mental, and—by quiet extension—the physical dimensions of life.

A Personal Journey of Healing

Ravi's personal journey of healing unfolded not through effort, but through attentive listening—an inward journey of self-exploration, where scattered fragments slowly found coherence, and grace created the space for him to rest deep within himself.

Every encounter unfolds somewhere—not merely on a map, but within a landscape shaped by memory, lineage, and quiet waiting.

Gurudev has transformed millions of lives through the breathing technique of Sudarshan Kriya and it is his grace as to how alcoholics and drug addicts have recovered from the ailment.

Gorakhpur is synonymous with the Gorakhnath Temple and Yogi Adityanath, the present Chief Minister of Uttar Pradesh.

Ravi had taken charge as Chief Operations Manager and Chief Commercial Manager of North Eastern Railway (headquartered at Gorakhpur). His first endeavor that first evening in Gorakhpur evening was to obtain a yoga mat to continue with his daily *sadhana.*

The long hunt across several shops culminated in a Divine shop of the Art of Living Foundation where an Advanced Meditation Course was being conducted by none other than Swami Surya Pada (a foremost teacher of the foundation). ***This was a classic case of belief and faith culminating into reality.*** Devotees and those present were taken aback as he and his wife were warmly greeted by Swamiji.

A little later, Ravi was informed by Kishoreda or Kishore Mukherjee (one of the first teachers of the foundation) that Gurudev and he were put up at the very same railway guest house and the very same room where Ravi was temporarily lodged.

This was yet another signature blessing of the Master and like a young child Ravi shared it with his mother who was absolutely ecstatic as to how the events unfolded at Gorakhpur.

As during all his earlier postings, Ravi touched base with the local chapter of the Art of Living and soon began conducting Sunday follow ups.

The news regarding Art of Living courses conducted for the front life staff and officers of the North Eastern Railways made waves and he was asked to address students at a prominent college in Izzatnagar, about his writings and official work and on courses of the Art of Living for railway personnel on prominent TV and radio channels in Delhi and Uttar Pradesh. The talks centred especially on the impact of Sudarshan Kriya to ameliorate stress on railway personnel while performing official duties.

A singular question posed was—while holding pivotal posts in the Railways, how was he was involved in Art of Living activities besides pursuing the passion of writing?

"This was purely because of the ***blessings of the Master, meditation, yoga and pranayama and the regular practice of Sudarshan Kriya,"* was his simple answer. And this is a reality. The bedrock of Gurudev's knowledge is: taking up responsibility empowers a person and the person can simply perform magic.***

All this culminated in some people contacting him to conduct courses for alcoholics and drug addicts at a rehabilitation centre in Gorakhpur.

So, a group of three Art of Living teachers conducted an introductory talk for alcoholics and drug addicts about the course at a rather bleak, gloaming, and desultory rehabilitation center. The energy levels at the center were abysmally low and they could palpably feel the negativity.

For some strange reason or the other the courses promised by them for the alcoholics and drug addicts did not take off. Official work, constant travel, and nonstop meetings were all contributory factors. This enfeebled Ravi immensely. He felt he was neglecting a part of his responsibilities. So much so, the delay took a toll on his health and he suffered physically and was enervated. His prana levels dipped and virtually began feeling ill all the time for no obvious reason.

It was at this juncture that the U.P. Apex body of the Art of Living stepped in and sponsored the course for the first batch of addicts. Subsequently the good Samaritan in Ravi's mother also funded few more courses for the addicts.

But once the addicts were exposed to the right techniques of yoga, pranayama, meditation, and Sudarshan Kriya they wept inconsolably like small children who were desperate to go back home to their near and dear ones.

This is the magnetic influence of Sudarshan Kriya as a flood of emotions swept away all negativity from their minds and thought process. Ravi could seamlessly connect with the addicts as he himself had been extricated from the very same cesspool.

This was his faith and belief that a miracle would occur.

This was a telling lesson in life for him as to how performing seva helps a person to evolve and grow in the divine manifestation of Pujya Gurudev.

✧ Keys to De-addiction

Do those dependent on alcohol have it in them to stay half-an-hour without alcohol?

Addicts need to upend the pyramid, detoxify their minds and bodies and once again discover love in their lives. It is paramount that they discard feelings and emotions of futility, guilt, inadequacy, and self-rejection. They have to strengthen their minds and make it robust to eschew dependency on alcohol.

Such craftsmanship and techniques are encompassed in the *Pragna* programme of the Art of Living and is providing succor to addicts. Various Art of Living programs address different sections of society to provide alternative and holistic therapies to ameliorate the physical and mental conditions of overwrought people.

How does one conduct the course for hardened alcoholics and drug addicts, who are in a perpetual state of self-denial? They look at the teacher in the most disgusted manner possible, with disbelief writ large on their faces.

Courses of the Art of Living for addicts need to be supplemented with regular follow-up sessions. The breathing technique of Sudarshan Kriya and the knowledge points of Gurudev begin to unfold, with a salutary impact on the minds of the addicts.

Slowly, the determination to metamorphose and transfigure their lives and eschew dependency on the substance begins to develop.

What really touches the heart is when an addict takes the first step. They break down as they seek help. *"Sir, aap humko chod kar jaoge toh nahin?"* (Sir, you will not forsake us?) *"Sir, aap roz aoge na?"* (Sir, will you come and meet us every day?) is the common refrain, as they develop a bond with the teacher.

The addict becomes determined to break the four walls of the rehab center.

Normally the mind of an alcoholic borders on futility, guilt, a gargantuan burden of inadequacy, self-rejection, self-depravation, and self-dejection. After the initial treatment at the rehabilitation center and subsequent exposure to the unique rhythmic breathing technique of Sudarshan Kriya they began to believe in the "Power of Now", the efficacy of "Living in the Present Moment".

Every day is a new day; a harbinger of hope and the addicts realize their self-worth and the "Power of Love and Acceptance" and begin giving themselves positive strokes.

The inmates of the center could remain half-an-hour without alcohol, can you? This is the question that resonates in Ravi's mind, the question he poses to any addict. The answer is simple; it is possible only through surrender to a higher power, the supreme intelligence of the Universe.

✧ Maharashtra De-Addiction Program

Despite the perils substance and alcohol abuse why do humans get addicted to these stimulants? The answer is always the same—a weak mind. The individual who is dependent on alcohol, drugs and other derivatives lives in a state of self-denial, dejection, self-deprecation, a feeling of absolute loss, loneliness and is looking for compassion, comfort, and love.

"Addiction is a brain disorder characterized by compulsive engagement in rewarding stimuli despite adverse consequences. The two properties that characterize all addictive stimuli are that they are reinforcing (i.e., they increase the likelihood that a person will seek repeated exposure to them) and intrinsically rewarding (i.e., they are perceived as being inherently positive, desirable, and pleasurable)." - Wikipedia

As per Hindu mythology, during the great churning process or *Amrit Manthan*, several jewels mushroomed (14 to be exact). Among them was *Varuni* – the Goddess of Wine.

Further, consumption of cannabis was known in India since 2000 B.C. It is associated with Lord Shiva, the Adi Yogi. But he was a mendicant who had mastered all the senses and was the suzerain of his mind. But the hapless addicts and alcoholics are victims of this deadly pestilence, succumbing to its ill effects. It has been proven statistically that nearly 15% of individuals who consume alcohol develop a dependency and, in the bargain, become alcoholics.

This is a major health problem, afflicting rich and poor alike. Further dependency on alcohol is associated with acute social stigma. There is nothing macho or brawny about it. This fatal attraction to alcohol deranges families and alcoholics get lost in the byzantine labyrinth of antipathetic thought process. Very often, they are discarded by loved ones and lead a life of ignominy.

The major categories of drugs which swamp the minds of addicts include alcohol, nicotine, tobacco, depressants like barbiturates and benzodiazepines, stimulants like amphetamines and cocaine, marijuana as well as opioids like morphine, heroin, and methadone.

Primarily such kind of addictions arise on account of peer pressure, poverty, impulsivity, relationship problems, family problems, poor coping skills among others.

Shri Venkatesh Manglaram, a senior faculty of the Art of Living has been an inspirational figure in weaning away addicts from this lethal pestilence through some landmark work and contribution.

Venkateshji opines that most of the participants gravitated towards such drugs on the assumption it might provide some handy solutions and some relief which triggers the human mind into obfuscating immediate problems, without realizing the immense damage it can cause to the human system.

Venkateshji put it succinctly, "When someone drinks alcohol or takes drugs and becomes dependent on it; their family suffers; the surrounding suffers and it overall affects the society. Since I am a part of the society, I feel responsible for the same."

The triumvirate of Venkatesh Manglaram, Nitin Pradhan and Ganshyam Gohile has conducted 23 *Prana* courses together which has upended the pyramid of around 330 addicts in the arid region of Vidharbha in Maharashtra.

The fulcrum of the *Prana* course is to stress on absolute detoxification; de-addiction is carried out with a holistic approach.

The course is a unique combination of physical, psychological, emotional, social and spiritual practices such as yoga, meditation, and imparting the unique rhythmic breathing technique of Sudarshan Kriya.

The course has had a stunning and astonishing strike rate, with as many as 80% participants eschewing dependency on alcohol and drugs.

The mind of an alcoholic or a drug addict swings like a pendulum. On one hand is the immediate feeling of euphoria and at the other end is an extremely enfeebled mind which is not robust enough to eschew the dependency. Thus, registration of individuals becomes a gargantuan task, the biggest stumbling block.

Once they complete the course the results are there to see; radiant faces and minds suffused with jollity. One such participant was Shrirang Jagtap, a resident of Amravati who was trained to be a civil engineer. However, he was tragically caught in the vortex of alcohol consumption.

In sheer desperation, the gentleman attempted various de-addiction courses at several places and was admitted at different rehabilitation centers but ended up only drinking, with no aperture of hope in sight.

Eventually, he attended a *Prana* course and it has been several years now that he is sober and clean. Yet another participant was Amol, a bus conductor in Yavatmal. He began consuming alcohol on account of certain family problems but ended up losing his job due to excessive drinking. The course has benefitted him in such a remarkable manner that presently he has been sober, without touching a drop for many years.

The duration of the course is such that the participants and teachers strike a chord and are able to empathize with each other. The afflicted can reach out to the teachers whenever they are desirous of giving vent to their feelings.

Upon completion of the course it is mandatory to conduct follow up sessions and *satsangs,* so that the recovered souls do not hurtle once again towards alcoholism or drug addiction.

The success rate of abstinence has been as high as 80%, no mean achievement!

In order to construct a *'NO ALCOHOL'* society, it is imperative that tools of education and large-scale awareness about the perils of alcoholism and addiction should be imparted.

Venkatesh and his team are working towards this lofty mission.

Reflection & Exercises:

- Reflect on someone whose guidance transformed your life.
- How can I be an instrument of positive change?

Personal Journal Page: Note your personal transformations.

Chapter 18

Peace and Reconciliation

Peace, as Gurudev Sri Sri Ravi Shankar envisions it, is not merely the absence of conflict—it is the presence of understanding, compassion, and inner stillness. It is not forged only through treaties or declarations, but discovered in the quiet reordering of the human heart. His work across the world affirms a profound truth: **when inner turbulence settles, the outer world begins to heal.**

Across continents—from the dense hills of Assam and the wounded valleys of Kashmir to the scarred landscapes of Iraq and the long-divided nation of Colombia—Gurudev has entered spaces burdened by fear, grief, and mistrust. Not as a negotiator armed with demands, but as a presence that listens, softens, and gently reminds people of their shared humanity.

When Violence Learns to Rest

In Assam's lush green terrain, conflict had long cast its shadow over families and futures. Among those caught in its grip was a young man who had once belonged to the United Liberation Front of Asom (ULFA). Like many others, his life had been shaped by fear, anger, and an exhausting vigilance. When he was invited to attend a trauma-relief and stress-management program under Gurudev's peace initiative, he arrived without expectation—

perhaps even with resistance.

What unfolded surprised him. Through breathwork, meditation, and structured dialogue, something within him loosened. The body released tensions it had carried for years; the mind discovered a stillness it had never known. When he returned home, he did not carry slogans or ideologies. He carried seeds.

He began organic farming, encouraged cooperative livelihoods, and slowly rebuilt trust within his community. The hands that once held weapons now tended soil. Over time, he emerged not as a former militant, but as a **custodian of peace,** guiding others toward sustainable, dignified living.

Healing Before Rebuilding

Conflict is not always marked by arms alone. In Assam, recurring floods have displaced families overnight, leaving behind not only material loss but deep psychological scars. In makeshift shelters and waterlogged fields, facilitators from Gurudev's trauma-relief programs arrived quietly—without promises of instant recovery.

They offered presence. Simple breathing practices. Gentle guided reflection. In one such gathering, an elderly woman who had lost her home and watched children sink into fear and silence later shared that it was the pause of inner calm—just a few conscious breaths—that restored her sense of agency. *"I cannot rebuild everything,"* she said, *"but I can sit with myself again."* These workshops did not erase suffering; they restored the strength to endure, adapt, and begin anew.

Paigam-e-Mohabbat: When Hearts Meet Before Positions

In the valley of Kashmir, where decades of sorrow had hardened identities, Gurudev's initiative *Paigam-e-Mohabbat*—the Message of Love—opened a space unlike any other. Families who had lost sons on opposing sides of the conflict sat in the same hall. Grief was raw, unfiltered. Husbands who had lost wives to cross-firing faced parents whose children had disappeared into violence.

What unfolded was not debate, but recognition. Tears replaced arguments. Apologies surfaced where blame once lived. In that shared vulnerability, hatred loosened its hold. The moment transcended politics; it marked an emotional turning point, reminding all present that **pain does not belong to one side alone.** Peace, in that hall, was no longer an abstraction—it was palpable, fragile, and deeply human.

From Inner Silence to National Healing: Colombia

Half a world away, Colombia had endured over five decades of armed conflict between the FARC guerrilla forces and the government. When negotiations reached an impasse, Gurudev was invited to engage with leaders and negotiators from both sides. His approach was characteristically quiet—reaffirming nonviolence, encouraging reflection, and gently guiding participants to see beyond entrenched positions toward shared humanity.

His presence helped create openings where dialogue had stalled. In 2016, the historic peace accord was signed in Cartagena, formally ending one of Latin America's longest conflicts. Yet the deeper work continued beyond the signing. In subsequent gatherings facilitated by The Art of Living, families who had lost loved ones stood alongside former combatants in forgiveness circles—hands joined, grief acknowledged, responsibility shared. This was not merely the end of a war; it was a **ceasefire within hearts.**

Rebuilding Hope Amid Ruins: Iraq

In Iraq, years of violence had fractured communities and eroded trust in daily life. Gurudev's peace initiatives here unfolded through trauma-relief programs, women's empowerment efforts, and community-centered education. Tens of thousands—

from Baghdad to Basra—found in meditation and stress-relief techniques a new way to process fear and loss.

For many women who had lost spouses or family members, these programs offered more than emotional solace. Livelihood training restored self-reliance; collective practices restored dignity. Participants spoke of laughter returning where despair once reigned, and of inner peace becoming the soil in which social recovery could take root.

Healing Through Presence

Francisco Moreno Ocampo, reflecting on his work alongside Gurudev, observes that peace is rarely negotiated into existence—it is *cultivated.* Through meditation and outreach among youth, he has witnessed how inner transformation becomes a social force. Breath softens hardened worldviews; stillness awakens responsibility. Meditation, he notes, is not an escape from reality, but a way of engaging it with clarity and compassion—preparing individuals not for conflict, but for coexistence.

Reconciliation at Home

In India, Gurudev's peace efforts have consistently followed the same rhythm: listen deeply, bring people together, and restore the ability to see one another as human. From facilitating dialogue during the Amarnath land dispute in Kashmir to working with displaced communities and former militants in the Northeast, this compassion-centered approach has supported surrenders of arms, reductions in violence, and renewed commitments to peaceful livelihoods.

A Civilizational Wound Finds Stillness: The Ram Mandir Reconciliation

Among the many conflicts Gurudev has engaged with, some are not measured in years, but in centuries. The Ram Mandir dispute—

nearly five hundred years old—was not merely a legal or political contention; it was a deeply layered civilizational wound, carrying the weight of history, memory, identity, and faith.

In the years leading up to its resolution, when tensions ran high and rhetoric threatened to eclipse reason, Gurudev quietly stepped into the role he has so often embodied—that of a *trustee of harmony*. Without seeking visibility, he offered counsel grounded in restraint, mutual respect, and the larger vision of social cohesion. His advisory presence emphasized that no lasting resolution could emerge from triumphalism or humiliation, but only from **dignity on all sides.**

Through patient dialogue with leaders across communities, Gurudev consistently underscored the importance of honoring faith without inflaming division, and of allowing the process to unfold through constitutional means rather than emotional escalation. His guidance helped reinforce a climate where restraint prevailed over provocation, and where the eventual resolution—achieved through legal and democratic processes—was received with calm rather than conflict.

What was remarkable was not merely that a centuries-old dispute found closure, but that it did so **without widespread violence,** allowing the nation to exhale rather than erupt. In that stillness lay a deeper reconciliation: an affirmation that even the most enduring historical fractures can be addressed when wisdom tempers passion, and when leadership chooses peace over polarization.

This moment stood as a quiet testament to Gurudev's consistent philosophy—that reconciliation is not about erasing differences, but about **holding them without hostility**, allowing time, trust, and collective maturity to do their work.

Why These Stories Matter

These journeys reveal that peace is not only signed into being—it is lived into being. Treaties may halt wars, but **healed hearts prevent their return.** Across all these contexts, a consistent philosophy emerges: inner stillness becomes the clay from which compassion, trust, and reconciliation are shaped.

Through patient dialogue, trauma relief, shared forgiveness, and invitations to self-reflection, Gurudev's work demonstrates that the path from conflict to peace is as much inward as it is outward. It is a path where breath becomes courage, compassion becomes strategy, and presence becomes the most enduring instrument of peace.

The Quiet Principles That Hold Peace

Across these varied landscapes—Assam's forests, Kashmir's valleys, Colombia's negotiating tables, Iraq's shattered neighborhoods, and India's ancient civilizational crossroads—there runs a quiet, unbroken thread. Gurudev's peace work is not driven by ideology or immediacy, but by a set of enduring principles that act less like strategies and more like *ethical bearings.*

At the heart of his approach lies **compassion without discrimination**—a willingness to see the human being before the label of victim or perpetrator. In rooms where anger once dominated, he has consistently invited empathy to enter, reminding all involved that suffering, when unattended, only multiplies itself. By addressing pain rather than assigning blame, he has helped soften hardened positions and reopen pathways to dialogue.

Equally central is **patience and deep listening.** Gurudev's interventions are marked by an unusual restraint—a refusal to rush resolution or impose outcomes. Whether in Kashmir, Colombia, or during India's most sensitive internal disputes, he has demonstrated that listening itself can become an instrument of reconciliation. In being heard, individuals and communities often rediscover their own capacity to step back from violence.

Yet compassion and listening are never left as abstractions. Gurudev's peace initiatives consistently translate insight into **empowerment**—through education, livelihood training, skill development, and trauma relief. Former militants learning organic farming, displaced families rediscovering emotional resilience, and women rebuilding self-reliance in war-torn regions all point to the same understanding: peace must be economically and socially sustainable to endure.

Underlying this work is a profound respect for **cultural, linguistic, and spiritual diversity.** Rather than seeing difference as a fault line, Gurudev treats it as a reservoir of richness. His peace efforts honor local identities while gently guiding communities toward shared human values, allowing unity to arise without uniformity.

Above all, there is a long view—a commitment to **solutions that outlast the moment**. Gurudev's engagement does not end with ceasefires or agreements; it continues through healing, education, and inner transformation. His emphasis on meditation and breathwork reflects a deep conviction: that peace imposed from outside is fragile, but peace cultivated within becomes self-sustaining.

Through decades of such engagement, Gurudev has shown that peace is neither distant nor abstract. It begins with understanding, matures through dialogue, and finds strength in the courage to meet violence not with retaliation, but with compassion. His work in Kashmir, the Northeast, and across the world stands as a living testament to the transformative power of presence—where wisdom replaces reactivity, and human values quietly reshape the future.

These principles do not remain confined to meditation halls or negotiating tables alone. They find expression in the lived realities of governance, administration, and service—often in places where peace must navigate difficult terrain, historical neglect, and complex human systems.

What follows is one such account, where the philosophy of inner peace meets the challenges of infrastructure, responsibility, and public life. Through the lens of lived experience, Gurudev's vision of reconciliation and presence quietly permeates the working of institutions and the hearts of those entrusted with service.

NFR Bound – In a Different Zone

The Northeast Frontier Railway (abbreviated NFR), is one of the 18 railway zones of the Indian Railways. It is headquartered at Maligaon, Guwahati in the state of Assam. It is responsible for operation and expansion of rail network all across North-eastern states and some districts of eastern Bihar and northern West Bengal.

This difficult terrain limits the rail network expansion. The network is not broad gauge in many parts and the rail lines are antiquated with speeds at some sections being limited to a maximum of thirty kilometers per hour.

So, with this geography of the area in his thoughts Ravi looked forward to take charge as the Chief Freight Traffic Manager (CFTM) North East Frontier Railway.

The enfeebled mind was once the enemy and alcoholism was a manifestation. This battle had to be won. Victory over the bottle was achieved once he learnt not to succumb to the weakness.

Once Ravi could discover the adversary, he fought it by practicing Sudarshan Kriya at the behest of his wife.

But above all it was the X-factor in form of the grace of the Master or Guru which played a decisive role in countering any physical, emotional, or psychological blockade which triggers a negative change.

Upon joining as CFTM, he was in a different zone altogether, both metaphorically and physically.

Now that the mandarins of the Traffic directorate of Railway Board, Ministry of Railways had zeroed-in on him to occupy this prominent post, it became incumbent to maintain his sobriety which was barely a year old. Every day of remaining sober and dry counted. A single slip would have sucked a person into the abyss once again.

He was fortuitously able to establish contact with an Art of Living Teacher, through a batchmate on the very day he had taken over the charge. ***To him, this was a miracle, which just happened effortlessly, in a jiffy.*** Thus, Ravi could identify a place to attend Long Sudarshan Kriya.

Evening falls early in the North-Eastern parts of India. As shadows were lengthening, one could feel the chill in the air. Ravi and his wife reached Pandu Ashram of the Art of Living.

The sun was sinking in the colossal Brahmaputra and they were suffused with amazing energy and positive feelings. Pandu Ashram is situated right on the banks of the Brahmaputra River.

The Ashram reminded them of old times Gurukul where young tutees were imparted esoteric skills by learned scholars. Often when he attended Long Kriya sessions at the Pandu Ashram, Ravi would ponder on the question as to why did he not learn Sudarshan Kriya earlier in his life. The trajectory would have been so different.

It was Gurudev and the Art of Living through Sudarshan Kriya which brought an element of sanity in his life. Faith and belief in the techniques were the harbinger of change which transformed Ravi's personality and it was nothing short of a miracle was performed.

Every Sunday along with his wife, Ravi would attend the Long Sudarshan Kriya at the Pandu Ashram and soon there were a sequence of breath-taking events which rendered them speechless. Divinity manifested in the most facile manner and miracles took place.

The Pandu Ashram was administered by one gentleman by the name, Bhanu Bhaiyya (he is now an evolved soul with the appellation Swami Bhavya Tej).

This bearded gentleman from Uttarakhand lived in a thatched roof and braved all the vagaries of the inclement weather through the practice of yoga, pranayama, meditation, Sudarshan Kriya and *seva*.

He looked like an attractive youngster with a chiseled body endowed with a long attractive mane and a beard. Ramrod straight back, he almost looked like a *rishi* of the yore walking straight out of our myths.

There was a wonderful, extremely positive aura around him. For some inexplicable reason he took a liking towards Ravi and used to interact with him after the Sunday Long Kriya

They confabulated on a variety of subject ranging from the mundane to the spiritual, from politics to religiosity, about the law-and-order conditions in the North East, to the problems faced in Assam and most importantly Guru stories.

The man described various facets of Gurudev, his deep commitment to humanity and the innate divinity as Ravi heard Bhanu Bhaiyya in rapt attention.

The brahmachari listened to Ravi's long winding story of dalliance with alcohol and subsequent recovery from alcoholism, the problem of fistula and about his parents and childhood with great interest.

He merely laughed aloud and remarked, *"Ab toh sab theek hai na Guru kripa sey."*

One Sunday morning, Bhanu Bhaiyya played the Long Kriya cassette after a session of Suryanamaskars and the yogic practice of Padma*sadhana* as designed by Gurudev.

All the participants were startled at the sound emanating from the cassette player. It sounded as if an individual who was totally inebriated was reciting the *Soham Soham* (the syllable used by Gurudev in Sudarshan Kriya) chants and we failed to maintain the pace.

The cyclical and rhythmic breathing process was getting disrupted and a few started sniggering. A few of them were startled about the rendition. It was like an intoxicated person reciting Sudarshan Kriya.

Bhanu Bhaiyya maintained his poise and composure and stopped playing the cassette and sprinted to his kutir.

After some tinkering with the tape recorder, he played the cassette again which settled us down and we were engulfed in profound silence and were deeply rested after completion of the session.

Ravi's inquisitive mind kept inquiring from Bhaiyya as to what had happened while playing the cassette in the first instance. He parried Ravi's queries and laughed.

"Guruji ke saanidhya mein yeh sab hota rehata hai. Bas unko pakad ke rakho," (All this happens under Guruji's grace and presence. Just hold on to him tightly)

What was most mystifying was that the batteries in the tape recorder were placed with both + ends touching (not + and – as it ought to have been), yet the cassette played. Everyone was stupefied on hearing this, but such is the power of the Long Sudarshan Kriya cassette that it played despite the batteries being wrongly placed.

"If the cassette is so potent, imagine how powerful is the Long Kriya. And Gurudev is none other than a divine personality. We are blessed to be amidst a supernatural one such as Him," Bhanu Bhaiyya added.

The administrator of the Pandu Ashram in the meantime set up a meeting between Ravi and a senior faculty of Art of Living in Guwahati. The mission was to counsel the Chief Manager of a leading hotel in Guwahati.

"Now begin with performing some *seva*," Bhanu Bhaiyya was to tell Ravi quite firmly.

As night fell and Guwahati was plunged in darkness, the senior faculty of the Art of Living and the railway man interacted with the alcoholic.

They made several visits and over a period of time, miraculously the gentleman stayed off liquor and cigarettes. This miracle occurred only through the narration of Guru stories.

One evening, once again Ravi accompanied the Art of Living teacher. He thought they were again going to visit the manager of the hotel. But to Ravi's surprise they took a detour and travelled through a narrow alley and were in a room.

What they saw petrified them and was most numbing. They were seeing some known and several unknown faces. They were none other than the top brass of ultras belonging to AASU, ULFA and some other dreaded militant organizations.

The teacher had been working with the members of these

dreaded organizations, performing yeoman service, and spreading Gurudev's message of universal love, peace, and harmony so that they would eschew violence, give up arms, and join the mainstream once again.

The group present raised their war cries, demanding freedom, sloganeering against the government and the persecution they faced under the rule an oppressive regime.

Very soon they were connected through a Skype call to the Bangalore Ashram and they spoke to Gurudev and after some dialogue and quiet persuasion by the Master, the terrorists agreed to undergo a rehabilitation program at the Bangalore Ashram where they were to eschew violence, be fully disarmed, learn techniques of yoga, pranayama, meditation, Sudarshan Kriya and perform seva.

The Ministry of Home Affairs and the Indian Army had sanctioned a program of rehabilitation of these personnel. It so happened that Ravi was tasked to organize the rolling stock to arrange for their transportation from the North East to Bangalore Ashram. It was an onerous responsibility to organize the rolling stock.

On the appointed day, a little more than two hundred sullen, dour, angry, and hostile rebels who were chained from head to toe, totally disarmed, boarded a train to the Bangalore Ashram of the Art of Living to undergo the rehabilitation program.

The terrorists were heavily escorted by army, para military, and police officials. As the train chugged out of the Kamakhya station some of them attempted to jump out the moving train and the entire exercise went in vain as there was a virtual pandemonium.

The railway man was roundly remonstrated by his bosses on NF Railway for participating in what they considered to be a foolhardy exercise. All his efforts of explanations went unheard and he was questioned by the top officials of the zone.

The pleas of NF Railway not to proceed with transportation were turned down by the mandarins of power in Delhi and this time the group boarded the train which chugged along the tracks to Bangalore.

The dreaded gun totting menacing men were a transformed lot after participating in the course which became the tipping point in their lives.

This was nothing but the grace of the Divine. These are nothing but positive vibrations and only an individual blessed with faith and belief can be a witness when miraculous events take place.

The Roots of Seva

The northeast region of India has had a long history of movements for autonomy on behalf of several ethnic groups.

Bhanu Bhaiyya was aware about Ravi's role in the journey and the transformation in the lives of these terrorists. He was extremely happy about the development and on Ravi's participation, albeit indirectly in the process.

After a couple of months, upon completing the Sunday Long Kriya, Bhanu Bhaiyya brought a few sheets of papers, he prayed to Gurudev and asked Ravi to sign at the places that he indicated. This was the Teacher's Training Course (TTC) Phase 1 form.

Sometime back in 2007, when some participants broke silence upon completion of the Advanced Meditation Course at Bangalore Ashram, Ravi was on the terrace of Vishalakshi Mantapam along with a course mate and his wife and daughter who had returned from Ooty to pick him up from the Ashram.

Suddenly a stranger walked up to Ravi and she remarked, "You are looking so bright and incandescent. I can foretell that one day you will become an Art of Living Teacher."

Back then he was befuddled by her remark. Many years later, as recently in 2022 when Gurudev visited Tamil Nadu, Ravi was to travel together with the same lady, a senior faculty member. She remarked, "Fifteen years ago I made a prophecy, do you recall?" This is journey of strange incidences, beliefs, faith, and miracles which can be appreciated only in divine reverie.

On the insistence of Bhanu Bhaiyya, Ravi filled up the form where the brahmachari had proposed Ravi's name as a candidate for TTC. Subsequently Ravi was in Bangalore Ashram to undertake Phase 1 of the TTC.

The fifteen days of training, spent at the Bangalore Ashram required immense, from four in the morning to twelve in the night. Yoga, pranayama, intense meditation sessions, Sudarshan Kriya, *seva, satsang* and most importantly a direct contact with Gurudev, all these were part and parcel of the training program.

Celebrating life with Divinity is an experiential feeling which cannot be described in words. No amount of carousing, no pleasure on the world, fame or sharing the stage with a celebrity can match the moments spent in the presence of Divinity.

Moments spent in Gurudev's *saanidhya* surpassed all and outshone everything else. ***The longing and pining to have his glimpse and meet him is unimaginable, unfathomable, and indescribable.***

For devotees Gurudev is none other than Lord Krishna or Lord Narayana, reborn after 5,710 years; who with his impish smile, soft voice, esoteric knowledge, profound wisdom and contact, passes on vibrations to the devotee, seeker, disciple, swami, *rishi,* celebrities, ultras, politicians, and any stock individual.

It is dedication on part of the seeker to expand his bowl of acceptance and receive the grace transmitted by the Master.

In the Ashram, everything gets dropped as Gurudev through his teachings only promoted happiness through various techniques of Art of Living.

During the courses two baskets were kept in all the sessions - a) drop all your worries and b) drop all botheration. Only when the participant dropped all worries and botheration would he or she blossom. Once a person is bereft of problems, he/she lives in the present moment and spreads waves of happiness.

All participants were cautioned to tread the path of *sattva* very carefully as only the chosen ones were nominated for this taxing course. Thus, a seeker had to necessarily overcome baser instincts of *rajas* and *tamas* and tune-in, to be at the same frequency as Gurudev to be eligible to be seated on *Vyasa Peetha* (as the sacred seat is referred to) from where the faculty of Art of Living would be an instrument to impart the profound and life changing knowledge.

"The processes are such in the Art of Living TTC, it's amazing, a blossoming of your personality. Just go for it!" says Gurudev.

This game changing experience of *sadhana, seva, satsang,* Sudarshan Kriya, meditation and silence was completed within a period of fourteen days and the participants were transformed personalities, shining like stars and had surrendered all their scars and wounds.

The transformation one undergoes through intense sessions of Sudarshan Kriya, pranayama, meditation, yoga and seva is to be seen to be believed. One is emboldened to transform society. Several participants in the course were to tell our teachers that TTC is tougher than the commando course a soldier in battle fatigues undergoes.

"One should walk like a King and be a humble servant," says Gurudev. This is essential for all teachers who sit on the Vyasa Peetha to impart the

wisdom."

"Ab toh railway afsar aadhe teacher ban gaye. Khoob seva karo, meditation karo, seva karo. Jai Guru Dev." (Now a railway officer has become half a teacher. It is necessary that you engage in plenty of meditation and participate in seva. Jai Guru Dev.

Bhanu Bhaiyya held Ravi tightly and uttered these words. He was in particular very happy for he had been instrumental in journey to the Teacher's Training program.

Ctrl+Alt+Del

Assam was meanwhile rocked by a series of terror-violence incidents. The IGP (Law and Order) was the railway man's batchmate who sought the services of The Art of Living to reach out the terror affected people.

We were four

They were four hundred

Hurt and Wounded

They were numbed and stunned

We approached with caution and the grace of the Master

To assuage their feelings and emotions

They were terror affected children and women

Terror-affected widows and their children were all kept in police custody in some camps. All the bread earners were either annihilated by bloodletting terrorists or had fled the state. A three-day *shivir* or camp was organized by the Art of Living in which simple techniques of pranayama and meditation were taught. Thereafter, the participants performed some *seva*, which was followed by a set of games specially designed for the distraught women who had lost their loved ones and for the orphaned children.

These 400 people virtually uttered not a word for almost a month once violence wrecked their lives. They looked at the teachers grimly with suspicion while some women spoke in hushed tones.

Once the candle of flame which sustained the family was extinguished, the lifeboat had sunk. They had no place to fasten their anchorage. "What could a self-help group do to our lives?" was a valid question in the minds of the widows and orphans.

At the end of the three-day breath, yoga and meditation workshop their lives were transformed. Torrential tears flowed from the blank eyes of women, who wept inconsolably and hugged each other. The games designed in the workshop turned out to be game changers in their lives.

It was like operating simple keys on the keyboard.

In that quiet recognition, something settles—leaving behind not answers, but a deeper knowing.

Ctrl+Alt+Del

Control yourself

Alter your thoughts

Delete all anger and negativity.

What follows is not merely a narration, but an invitation into a lived moment of grace.

The negative emotions file in the computer of the mind was erased and the corrupted file was cleansed. Those were indeed satisfying and fulfilling moments of performing *seva*.

But were we doing the *seva*? The answer is a plain no, as we were only instruments and it was essentially the grace of the Master which was operating and resolving the misadventure encountered by the left-over members of the family.

Satsang hastens the seeker to inner peace. "In *satsang*, both the left and right hemispheres of the brain get balanced. The wandering mind comes back to the present moment and experiences a deeper dimension to life," explains Gurudev Sri Sri Ravi Shankar.

"The word *bhajan* is very precious. *Bhaj* means to share, sharing all that the divine. It is not necessary to know the words or meaning to any song. Singing helps to bring serenity.

Sound is energy. Our human nervous system responds to the sounds *bhajans* and vibrations of ancient Sanskrit chants. Listening to these sounds has a rejuvenating effect on the body, mind and spirit."

Gurudev provided us with a wonderful opportunity to organize a *satsang* to be conducted by a brilliant singer and senior faculty of the Art of Living, none other than Vikram Hazra. Vikram Hazra is like a finely cut diamond with multiple facets, each distinct yet collaborating to sparkle.

Vikram was once a journalist and when he filed a story on the AoL, his curiosity got the better of him and he ended up doing the basic course. It is a matter of great pride for this Indian spiritual rock star that people groove to his music at bars in places like Argentina and on those days, liquor is not served. This is once again nothing but the spiritual prowess of Gurudev.

Ravi had a fortuitous meeting with Vikram Bhaiyya at Pandu Ashram. He was full of positive energy and effervescence and regaled us with numerous Guru stories. A devotee was to tell me, "Vikram is indeed the apple of Gurudev's eye."

A fleeting greedy thought flitted across Ravi's mind. I wish to become someone like Vikram Bhaiyya. Someone close to the Master.

"Ravi, can you feel the energy and vibrancy of this place. Ages ago *rishis* and *munis* have all performed arduous tapas at this place," he remarked.

The spiritual rockstar soon began strumming his guitar and broke into a soulful number

In that quiet recognition, something settles—leaving behind not answers, but a deeper knowing.

Raadhe, Radhe Radhe Shyam

Govindaa Gopalaa Radhe Radhe Shyam

It was an ethereal experience which transported all of us to divine ecstasy. The back-to-back *satsangs* by Vikram Hazra were a big draw as people and devotees of Shillong and Guwahati grooved to the music.

For some strange reason Ravi struck a chord with this brilliant musician and mellifluous singer. He also got an opportunity to compere his programme at Guwahati.

The Blast

The symphony spun by Vikram Hazra was shattered by the cacophony which rocked North East Frontier Railway headquarters office.

A blast killed several railway personnel. Apparently, the terrorists had planted the bombs in the two-wheelers and cycles of innocent railway-men parked outside the office. Ravi's driver rushed him home and advised him not to go for the customary evening walk. Section 144 was clamped.

A few days later, at the suggestion of an Art of Living devotee and Member of Parliament from Shillong, a *satsang* and meditation session was organized in the railway auditorium.

This was a welcome move as a large number of railway families who were all locked indoors for almost ten days, stepped out to take part in the celebrations.

The session included videos on Gurudev, the work of the Art of Living teachers under the guidance of Gurudev in the terror afflicted places, a *satsang,* breathing exercises, and a session of meditation. This had a salutary impact and several railway personnel enrolled for the Art of Living courses to learn the unique breathing technique of Sudarshan Kriya.

The district administration, police and railway administration were entirely thankful to the organization for undertaking this unique seva. We were to witness yet another manifestation of the Guru's grace and *kripa.*

Ravi witnessed faith transforming into a miracle. This was once again tasting the ambrosia of Glimpses of Grace.

Mai Tera, Tera Main

Gurudev always jokes about the implication of his birthday being on 13 May. 13th May, in Hindi reads as Tera Mai(n). Gurudev ingenuously flips this around to call it Mai(n) Tera…meaning I am yours.

Pandu Ashram at Guwahati, like all other Art of Living ashrams was decked up and teeming with faithful devotees. The day began with several pujas invoking the divine power and seeking blessings from the Almighty. This was followed by Guru Puja which is so special as it is the Guru who opens the doors to the Lord. Thereafter teachers conducted yoga, pranayama, and meditation sessions and then the army of devotees embarked upon cleaning and sweeping the streets of Guwahati as part of *seva*, feeding the hungry and planting trees as part of clean and green Guwahati project.

But everyone was waiting with bated breath for the evening session which included the Long Sudashan Kriya and to be followed by *satsang* and *prasadam*.

Very soon the assemblage was in deep rest after Long Sudarshan Kriya, totally refreshed. By now it was dark as the sun had set. Only the last leg of the program, which was the *satsang* remained. After that devotees would have *prasadam* and the program would conclude.

Pandu Ashram is situated on hilly terrain. While the main *Yagnyashala* or hall is at the lowest level, the rest of the structures are situated at increasing elevation, on three different levels.

As a result, the topmost structure which was Gurudev's *kutir* overlooked the entire complex. All the beautiful white buildings were decked out in fairy lights and against the dark night time background looked magical. In fact, this was the sight devotees saw as they emerged from the deep slumber after the Long Sudarshan Kriya. Suddenly, there seemed to be a wave of excitement which seemed to pick up momentum.

As devotees were attempting to capture the beautiful surroundings, some of them were amazed when the white structures against the night sky appeared in their phones as the silhouette of a bearded man in flowing white robes. This was incredible. They were aware that Pujya Gurudev was at Buenos Aires on May 13th for the birthday celebrations that year. So, the question was how Gurudev Sri Sri Ravi Shankar had appeared in Pandu Ashram?

The joy and happiness of the devotees present at the Ashram knew no bounds. Devotees felt that Gurudev had specially blessed them. It took a while before Bhanu Bhaiyya silenced all by loudly proclaiming, "Jai Gurudev" and brandished the mobile phone and directed the present devotees to pay their obeisance to the Master. This was followed by a grand *satsang* where everyone present was immersed in the blanket of positivity.

On closer look of the photograph, it was apparent that Gurudev was seated just behind a white curtain and one wonders for how long his astral body and spirit was present at Pandu ashram though physically he was at Buenos Aires.

Interacting with Gurudev at Itanagar

Founded in 2006, the Art of Living Ashram in Jully Basti, midway between Itanagar and Naharlagun is the headquarters of Art of Living in Arunachal Pradesh.

The ashram is a perfect place for spiritual practice. Way back in 2008 the Itanagar Ashram was being manned by Bhanu Bhaiyya, who had moved there from the Pandu Ashram.

Ravi's wife had enrolled for the Advanced Meditation Course. For most people attending the course, it was just an opportunity to be in the presence of Gurudev, rather than actually maintain silence. While most participants in the course were running after Gurudev, a few, including his wife were deeply immersed in the Advanced Meditation Course. ***The belief and faith in Gurudev and in his teachings is more than adequate for miracles to take place and one.***

People in hordes from all parts of the North East descended on Itanagar to have a glimpse of the Master. And when people are in multitudes it is always efficacious to be blessed with positive connections.

What are Connections?

Still half a teacher and railwayman, Ravi was blessed to suddenly discover two such connections. One in Vikram Hazra, the man with a golden voice and the other the senior faculty of Art of Living from Kolkata (the very same teacher who had prophesized that he would become an Art of Living faculty one day). These connections helped him and his family to have Gurudev's *darshan* several times.

If one is not feeling close to the Guru, it is because of one's own perceptions and predilections. "Because of our vacillating mind, on account of our ego concepts we lose the connection with the Master,' Bhanu Bhaiyya was to say.

Gurudev says, "Share with the Guru that which is very important or intimate to you. Share that. Do not feel shame, shy, or judgmental about yourself." "Unless you express to the Master that which is very intimate and important to you, just being on the formal and informal communication levels cannot make you feel close."

'If you don't feel close to the Master, there's no point in having a Master. It is just another burden to you. You have enough already. Just say goodbye, get rid of it."

Devotees were all stunned when divinity just passes by you like a cloud or touches a person so calmly and gently. The person feels numbed and as light as a feather. The mind is flooded with positive emotions; the heart beats rapidly and only tears of gratitude flow torrentially. It is well-nigh impossible to verbalize with the Master and one can only graciously accept his blessings and feel the vibrations and energy he passes by.

It seemed like eternity when Ravi along with his son and daughter were in the Divine aura of the Master in a small room at the Itanagar Ashram. Gurudev was looking radiant, neatly attired in a dhoti, kurta, and shawl and had a rosary in his hands with his trademark flowing mane. His bright eyes pierced them. They bowed before the Master, touched his feet, but could barely utter any word. The trio remained speechless and transfixed at their seats. No word uttered, nothing spoken only divine vibration was the medium of communication.

A smiling Gurudev offered chocolates to Ravi's children. These are of Chinese make," he laughed. There was so much that Ravi was desirous of asking Gurudev but was rendered speechless. His throat was parched and Gurudev was quietly observing them and smiling.

But he disarmed them, *"Kaise ho tum sab log?* How are you all?" These words were so comforting. Memories of those twenty to twenty-five minutes spent alone with Guruji, with just his children totally undisturbed, while Ravi's wife was going through the processes of Advanced Meditation Course will forever remain etched in the alcoves of their minds.

There are millions of devotees of Gurudev across the globe and here Ravi and his children spent quality time with Master all alone as he illuminated them with immense positive vibrations, thoughts, and energy.

They were all were in deep silence just covered by the blanket of love, affection, compassion of Gurudev. "What more could a follower ask for?" Ravi thought aloud.

The year was 2008 when Ravi received the call letter for Teacher's Training Course (TTC) Phase 2. This course is mandatory for an individual to become part of Art of Living faculty. He had applied for twenty-one days leave-against-pay (in government parlance LAP), but it was shot down by the local administration. No amount on entreaties and placatory supplications could convince his superiors, who were bent upon torturing him.

Persistence

While fervently praying to Gurudev, Ravi had sounded the top honchos of Railway Board about his proposed trip to Bangalore Ashram.

And then the miracle happened. The suzerains of NF Railway were categorically informed that leave had to be granted.

Fortuitously his bandwidth with the officers in Railway Board was on a different plane, unlike the trust deficit which he faced with his superiors at the zonal headquarters.

Officials at Railway Board were aware as to how he had battled with alcoholism and regained sobriety through the Art of Living programs. He headed for Bangalore Ashram after a brief stop to see his parents. He arrived at the Ashram running temperature, to undergo the TTC Phase 2 course.

The first few days were quite a challenge as he was struggling with the abdominal bug, but finally overcame the pestilence. With a hectic schedule of *sadhna, seva, satsang* and the stomach ailment he had lost quite a bit of weight, but like a brave warrior kept soldiering on with the grace of the Master.

Encounter with the Master

TTC Phase 2 was in full swing. Ravi realized that the power-packed programme included an absolute surrender to the Guru, to the Master.

But there were a few stand outs in the course which were truly path breaking and his conscience was in 100% agreement.

After the *satsang,* in a divine reverie Gurudev normally floats away to his *kutir* or some other place for a small meal or to meet someone. But for a strange reason, one evening during the course, the ***Master stayed on, and was perhaps waiting for someone.***

"He is waiting for you. Muster the necessary courage and go and speak up and share your problem. If you cannot surrender and share

your problems, disturbances, botheration with the Master what is the point of having one," Ravi's conscience goaded him. But Ravi could not muster adequate courage to go up to Gurudev.

A few days later, once the *satsang* was over, Gurudev was toying with a garland and playing with it as he placed it on a Nataraja statue at Vishalakshi Mantapam. Ravi finally mustered courage and rushed on to the stage and went straight to Gurudev as a stunned audience on.

Gurudev's secretaries tried to prevent him from tearing into the fold of the Master, but he disarmed all of them and signaled Ravi over towards him and asked him to speak up.

"Gurudev, the General Manager and officers of the railway have been repeatedly sending messages, ringing up and sending fax messages that I return back to Guwahati," Ravi blurted out.

"Complete your training and return," said the Master and levitated away as strains of the *bhajans* resonated at Vishalakshi Mantapam.

The General Manager of the Railway was singularly offended with Ravi as he had managed to attend the TTC using his contacts in the Railway Board. Despite Gurudev's simple and direct message to go back to Guwahati after completing the training, his mind was cannonaded with antipathetic and confused thoughts.

He was to send messages to his wife and mother, who were both surprised and vexed and asked him to have faith in Gurudev's words and allow the miracle to occur.

The TTC reached its summit and upon completion of the course the successful participants were given two precious gifts by Gurudev Sri Sri Ravi Shankar, the Teacher's Manual and the Sudarshan Kriya cassette.

They had all stumbled into infinity and were to share this

invaluable knowledge with the world and had joined the army of teachers to spread waves of happiness.

Reflection & Exercises:

- Consider conflicts in your life and how mindfulness could resolve them.
- What is your role in fostering harmony?

Personal Journal Page: Note your reflections on peace-building.

Chapter 19

Walking the Talk

There is a quiet authority that arises when life itself becomes the teaching. Gurudev Sri Sri Ravi Shankar embodies this authority effortlessly—not through assertion, but through alignment. When words and action spring from the same inner clarity, respect follows naturally. Faith, too, arises without being asked for. As Gurudev often observes with characteristic simplicity, when one lives what one speaks, trust is given freely; when one does not, no amount of insistence can earn it.

For Gurudev, leadership begins not in command, but in **self-mastery.** He often points out that before one attempts to influence the world, one must first tend to one's own inner state. A restless, agitated mind cannot offer clarity to others. This is why he places such emphasis on meditation—not as retreat from responsibility, but as preparation for it. Inner stillness, he reminds seekers and leaders alike, is not passivity; it is the ground from which right action emerges.

Humility as Inner Freedom

Those who encounter Gurudev for the first time are often surprised—not by the grandeur, but by an ordinariness and simplicity infused with depth. Despite decades of global engagement, his manner remains unencumbered by status. He moves easily among people, unguarded, attentive, and deeply human. Humility, in his presence, is not an act of lowering oneself—it is the absence of self-importance.

Once, after a long day of travel and public engagements, Gurudev quietly joined volunteers stacking chairs after an event. When someone tried to stop him, pointing out that others could do the task, he smiled and said softly, "If the body is there, let it help." In that simple gesture, leadership was redefined—not as privilege, but as participation.

He often reminds people that ego is not pride alone; it is also rigidity. A leader, he says, must remain flexible—willing to listen, willing to learn, willing to change course. This openness keeps intelligence alive and compassion awake.

Accessibility as Strength

Gurudev's accessibility is one of the most striking aspects of his leadership. Whether engaging with students, professionals, or heads of institutions, he creates a space where questions can be asked freely and differences expressed without fear. He listens fully—often before responding, sometimes choosing silence over immediacy.

In one interaction with young seekers, when asked how to command respect, he did not speak of authority, hierarchy, or influence. Instead, he spoke of **consistency**—that respect grows when actions are steady, intentions are clear, and conduct remains the same whether one is observed or alone. Leadership, he suggested, is less about being followed and more about being *trustworthy*.

He frequently emphasizes that clarity of mind allows one to communicate without aggression, to correct without humiliation, and to guide without control. A calm leader, he notes, can handle disagreement without hostility and pressure without panic.

Ethics Lived in Daily Choices

Gurudev's understanding of ethical leadership rests on a simple but demanding truth: **means are as important as ends.** He often cautions that when shortcuts are taken, the cost appears later—in erosion of trust, fatigue of spirit, or collapse of credibility. Integrity, in his view, is not situational; it is continuous.

This philosophy is evident in how he engages with institutions and public life. Though invited into many spaces of power, he remains advisory rather than authoritative. He facilitates dialogue, then steps back. He plants seeds of reconciliation, then allows others to nurture them. Credit is neither sought nor claimed. What matters is that harmony is restored.

He often remarks that when service is mixed with ego, exhaustion follows—but when service flows from clarity and compassion, energy renews itself. Those around him observe this paradox daily: despite relentless schedules, his presence remains light, playful, and alert. His tirelessness seems to arise not from force of will, but from inner alignment.

Small Gestures, Lasting Ripples

Some of the deepest teachings appear in moments too small to be recorded.

A volunteer once apologized for offering a very simple meal during a demanding day. Gurudev ate quietly and later said, "Food given with love is always complete." Another recalls him noticing a tired face in a crowd and asking, "Did you rest well?"—a question that dissolved distance in an instant.

Such moments do not announce themselves as lessons. Yet they leave impressions far deeper than discourse. They teach kindness without instruction, humility without doctrine.

When Life Becomes the Message

Because Gurudev lives the principles he speaks of, his influence multiplies beyond his own presence. People who work with him begin to lead differently—listening more, reacting less, serving without seeking recognition. Young people discover that strength does not require hardness, and authority need not silence compassion.

Walking the talk, in Gurudev's life, is not an effort—it is a natural consequence of inner stillness and resoluteness. This is why respect gathers around him quietly, why faith arises without persuasion, and why his presence inspires responsibility rather than dependence.

In a world that often celebrates words, Gurudev reminds us—through his life—that transformation follows those who live with coherence. When thought, word, and action move as one, leadership ceases to be a role and becomes a way of being.

And from such a life, ripples of love and selflessness continue to spread—unforced, enduring, and quietly transformative.

Eventually, after the words fall away, there is nothing to proclaim. What remains is presence. A life lived in quiet coherence, where thought, word, and action move as one, leaves behind no noise—only resonance. Gurudev's journey reminds us that the deepest teachings are not delivered; they are absorbed. In his stillness, one learns courage. In his humility, one discovers strength. And in the way he walks—lightly, tirelessly, without claiming—one understands that truth needs no announcement. It simply is. As the dust of words settles, what lingers is a gentle invitation: to live more honestly, to serve more freely, and to allow our own lives to become the message.

Some lives are not meant to be explained, only encountered.

When thought, word, and action move in quiet harmony, they leave behind no imprint of effort—only a gentle resonance. Gurudev's life reminds us that the most profound teachings are not spoken aloud; they are received in silence, absorbed through proximity, and lived through example. In his stillness, courage awakens. In his humility, strength finds its truest form. And in the way he walks—unencumbered, tireless, without claim—one recognizes that truth does not announce itself. It simply abides.

This, then, is offered not as a conclusion, but as a moment of pause—

with gratitude for the grace witnessed,

with reverence for a life lived in service,

and with a quiet prayer that such presence may continue to guide hearts,

long after these words have rested into silence.

Reflection & Exercises:

- Identify areas in life where actions align—or misalign—with values.
- How can integrity and humility guide my daily choices?

Personal Journal Page: Track your efforts at living principles authentically.

Part 6: Eternal Legacy – Gurudev's Message for Generations to Come

Chapter 20

Beyond Time and Space

Some lives belong to their moment.

Some shape an era.

And some move quietly ahead of time,

leaving footprints for generations yet to arrive.

This is not a conclusion.

It is a handover.

There are teachers who speak to the world as it is.

And there are Masters who speak to what the world is becoming.

Gurudev speaks from a place untouched by urgency.

His words do not chase relevance, nor cling to tradition.

They rest—steady, spacious—where truth has always waited.

He reminds humanity of something both ancient and immediate:

that peace is not constructed,

it is remembered.

Across languages and landscapes, his message arrives without resistance.

Not as doctrine.

Not as demand.

But as recognition—

a quiet yes within the listener.

He does not ask the world to slow down.

He teaches it how to move without losing its center.

Again and again, the same simplicity unfolds:

Change begins where awareness awakens.

Stillness is not escape, but source.

Joy is not earned; it is uncovered.

Compassion is not weakness, but intelligence.

In a time of fractured attention and restless becoming,

his teachings gather the human being back into wholeness—

breath by breath,

choice by choice,

moment by moment.

For generations raised amid speed and noise,

his message carries reassurance:

you are not lacking;

you are only distant from your own depth.

For leaders standing at crossroads of consequence,

he offers no formulas—only clarity.
For a planet weary of extraction and excess,
he restores reverence,
beginning within.
This is why his work cannot be contained by institutions or timelines.
It moves where hearts soften,
where silence is trusted,
where service flows naturally from joy.
Beyond time and space, the message remains unchanged:
When consciousness rises,
conflict loosens its grip.
When the heart remembers itself,
the future shifts.

Reflection & Exercises:

- ➢ Reflect on teachings that transcend your personal limitations or cultural boundaries.
- ➢ Which timeless principle can guide you today?

Personal Journal Page: Write your personal commitments to embody timeless wisdom.

Chapter 21

A Master's Blessing

A Master's blessing is not always spoken.

Sometimes it arrives as silence.

Sometimes as laughter.

Sometimes as a sentence that lingers for years, revealing new meanings with every life phase.

Across decades, Gurudev's words—often offered casually, almost playfully—have carried a precision that meets people exactly where they stand. Not to impress, instruct, or overwhelm, but to **unburden.**

He reminds us:

> *"Do not make your mind a burden to yourself."*
>
> *"Wisdom is knowing what to ignore."*
>
> *"Happiness is not dependent on what happens outside."*

These are not motivational lines; they are **keys**—simple enough to remember, deep enough to live a lifetime.

At milestones of personal and collective significance—beginnings, endings, moments of crisis or transition—his blessings often take the form of reassurance rather than promise. He does not tell people that life will be easy. He reminds them that **they are larger than life's fluctuations.**

To the anxious, he offers ease.

To the grieving, perspective.

To the ambitious, humility.

To the weary, rest.

And to all, without exception, he offers trust—trust in one's own inner intelligence.

What distinguishes his blessings is their refusal to create dependence. A true Master does not bind followers to himself; he returns them to themselves. Again and again, Gurudev redirects attention inward—not as an escape from responsibility, but as its rightful source.

His presence conveys what words cannot fully capture:

that one can be deeply engaged in the world without being

entangled,

that one can act decisively without aggression,

that one can love without possession,

and lead without domination.

For those who have encountered him—even briefly—there is often a subtle aftereffect: a loosening of urgency, a softening of inner noise, a renewed capacity to smile at complexity.

This, perhaps, is the Master's greatest blessing—not answers, not certainty, but **lightness.**

As this book rests into completion, what remains is not a portrait of a person, but an invitation—a quiet nudge toward stillness, service, and sincerity.

A blessing that does not end here, but continues wherever breath is taken consciously, wherever kindness is chosen over reaction, wherever silence is honored as wisdom.

And so, without proclamation or finality, the Master's message continues—

not written in pages, but lived in lives yet to unfold.

Reflection & Exercises:

➢ Note the blessings or guidance received in life over the years.

Personal Journal Page: Record the impact the blessings you have received have had on your life.

EPILOGUE - THE X-FACTOR

Victory to the Big Mind (Jai Guru Dev)

To anyone who is agitated, apprehensive, or discomposed I would recommend reading the Bhagavad Gita over and over again. As they pore into this masterpiece surely and certainly, they will find answers to their innumerable queries.

A peerless and invaluable conversation had taken place between Krishna and Arjuna eons ago. The Song Celestial is a potent message as relevant today as it was prior to the battle of Kurukshetra.

Lord Krishna deftly assuages the foggy and shadowy mind of his *sakha* Arjuna, so that the latter could discern between pusillanimity and alacrity and seize the opportunity to make his mind robust and brawny and thus fulfil his dharma, overcoming his personal feelings.

Today the minds of youngsters are cannonaded with innumerable choices. Presented with too many choices on the platter, many find they are unable to make the correct decision; be it the choice of career or their soulmate. Further the mind is constantly fusilladed by social media that they become addicted to gizmos and unduly smitten by the razzmatazz. In the process rationality in their choices is the first casualty.

This has become an endemic problem spanning across generations. Technology and alternatives have changed the paradigm and the ability to make rational decisions. The human mind is a victim of continuous bombardment and is never in the present moment to view things from the prism of objectivity.

The febrile and wavering mind which is never in the present moment and perpetually swinging like a pendulum between the past and the present is struck by certain feelings and emotions; feelings of attachment, entanglements, lust and obsession, greed and jealousy, anger and arrogance.

Apart from this the mind is gripped by the fear of the unknown. "What would happen

to me? "I am not feeling well," "How long will it take for me to recuperate," "Will I perform well in the examinations," "How will I fare in the interview" "Am I ready to make a pointed presentation which would impress the management and the customers," "Am I looking presentable to impress the girl next door," and so on... The list is endless. The mind is cannonaded by such thoughts. It does not provide the aperture to accept efficacious and positive thoughts.

The contributory reasons for negative thoughts are our low prana, qui or energy levels and lack of self-confidence.

It is like Lionel Messi, Neymar or Cristiano Ronaldo in the cauldron, where rambunctious crowds are rooting for them, and they miss a spot kick much to the consternation of the maniacal crowds and his team mates. Why does the mind freeze? Individuals are unable to perform. This could be due to lack of self-belief, overconfidence or just being unable to cope with the enormous pressure.

In various Art of Living programs, participants bow down to the angels of East, South, West and North to overcome emotions like attachments, entanglements, lust, obsessions, greed, jealousy, anger, and arrogance.

In the Happiness Program of the Art of Living, a precise and a special "Hum" technique is taught where in the individual release's fearful feelings and perturbation by literally screaming, "Hum". This releases all pent-up emotions.

As per Gurudev, the Mother Goddess had slain the asuras (demons) by bellowing "Hum". So, when an individual's mind is gripped by fear, it would be propitious to exercise the "Hum" technique rather than swallowing an anti-anxiety pill like Zapiz or Prozac.

Sudarshan Kriya, the unique rhythmic breathing technique brings the mind to the present moment. This brings awareness and mindfulness in an individual. Now before practicing Sudarshan Kriya, the seeker expresses gratitude to parents (our first teachers), ancestors (because of whom we are on this planet), to Mother Earth (which nourishes and sustains us), to the Sun God (which provides us light and energy) and finally to the Masters of the past, present and future who have imparted this repository of knowledge. Those who practice Sudarshan Kriya express their deep gratitude to Gurudev Sri Sri Ravi Shankar who has gifted humanity with this unique breathing technique and the profound knowledge.

Thus, Guru is the X–factor, the embodiment of Supreme Knowledge which metamorphoses and transfigures the mind. The Guru Tattva encompasses the Shiva Tattva and Narayana Tattva.

In the Mahabharata the Kaurava and Pandava armies braced themselves for the battle of Kurukshetra, to decide who would be the rightful heirs to the throne of Hastinapur.

The conceited and hubristic Duryodhana, egged on by his uncle, Shakuni and brother, Dushasana refused to enter into any treaty with their estranged cousins, the Pandavas. Thus, battling it out to don the prized crown was the only method to settle the contentious issue.

As the armies faced each other, before the conch was blown to signal the commencement of war, the ace archer, Arjuna quite inexplicably requested his charicteer, Lord Krishna, to take him closer to the enemy army so that he could have a close sight of his rivals.

The opponents consisted of the venerable Bhishma, his Gurus, Dronacharya and Kripacharya, and a hundred cousins.

Beholding the sight, Arjuna's mind was stricken with grief, remorse and guilt and he lay down his fabled arms and was of the opinion that it would be iniquitous to gain the lost kingdom by slaying his kinsmen. So much so he opined that the act could be termed as sinful and impious.

As if struck by a seizure, Arjuna was mentally distraught and willing to be annihilated rather than embark upon the voyage of bloodshed to avenge the ignominy of exile, the disrobing of Draupadi and the machinations of the evil Shakuni to usurp their kingdom. Such was the fragmented condition of Arjuna's mind.

Lord Krishna rebukes Arjuna for such a pusillanimous attitude and thoughts. There upon he exhorts Arjuna to raise the cudgels and embark upon the battle, as his mind ought to focus only on "doing the action, which was worthy of a Kshatriya" and not delve upon the purported consequences.

A true Yogi is one who is blessed with a brawny and robust mind, focused with steely determination to execute the task on hand fearless of the consequences.

But herein lies the catch. A resolute and authentic Yogi is one who is the sovereign of his mind. He does not get ensnared by cravings, lustful thoughts, unwelcome desires, and fearful thoughts but conquers his mind, attitudes and attains three inestimable qualities that is equilibrium, equipoise, and equanimity.

Lord Krishna thereupon reveals the secrets of life and death. The soul is indestructible and incombustible. The physical form which animate bodies assume is verily ephemeral. It is the soul which transmigrates from an individual to another. The human mind which is so precious should discern and grasp this aspect. In fact, Lord Krishna chastises valorous Arjuna for not adhering to the tenets of Karma Yoga, instead succumbing to filial ties. He added that "there is no purpose in grieving for the dead and the gates of heaven would welcome you with open arms."

The Lord further mentioned that even if Arjuna did not vanquish his adversaries, defeat would be equally glorious as he would have performed a deed befitting a warrior.

An intrepid mind, a warrior is one who takes up challenges and responsibilities and does not shirk from them. Taking up responsibility empowers an individual. This is true of anyone who is in pursuit of truth.

It is a weak and meek mind whose thoughts get obfuscated by the clouds of doubt.

Non–action is an act of cowardice too. Thus, it is essential for humans to act. For this purpose, it is essential that the human mind is trained to respond to various situations and not get stuck in the cesspool of inactivity.

A sagacious person, a true Karma Yogi discovers Divine peace in actions performed and is not bothered with the fruits of the action. The mind of such a person is pristine and the Yogi dwells in the body as a pure as the mind.

The Bhagvad Gita is the Song Celestial, running into 18 chapters; a memorable dialogue between Narayana and Nara (Arjuna). The Lord revealed his splendorous, luminous, and radiant form to Arjuna which encompassed the entire creation and destruction of the Universe. It is believed that Oppenheimer, the noted German physicist had similar visions when the first trial atomic test had taken place in the USA which is recorded in the book *Brighter Than a Thousand Suns* and more recently in the movie *Oppenheimer.*

More importantly, the sheer ferocity of the Vishwaroop Darshan of the Lord dispelled all doubts in the mind of Arjuna who was a transformed personality. His mind was at peace and all the cobwebs and demonic thoughts were torpedoed. He blew his conch "Devadutta" and strung the fabled "Gandiva" which sent shivers down the spine of his adversaries.

The mind of the bowman was truly awakened, aware, and rejoiced with joy as he was prepared for the battle. It is noteworthy to point out that the intrepid combatant had won from both within and without.

In our most impenetrable situations, it is only pristine knowledge which provides succor. The hallmark of a true Karma Yogi is to steadfastly remain in the state of this knowledge.

Only an authentic and genuine seeker, whose mind is hollow and empty bereft with all prejudices and preconceived notions is able to accept this knowledge and act upon it.

Thus, Guru is the X-factor who imparts knowledge to a genuine seeker at his feet.

"The Master's presence is not measured in moments, but in the endless echoes of grace."

— Gurudev Sri Sri Ravi Shankar

End Note: Echoes Beyond the Telling----- From Time Immemorial to 70 and to Infinity – He is all pervading

Even after the chapters have unfolded, the stories of Gurudev Sri Sri Ravi Shankar never truly end. His life and teachings are a river whose flow cannot be contained within the banks of a single book. What follows is not a conclusion, but an offering—an additional bouquet of untold moments, fragrant with grace, luminous with delight, and resonant with reverence.

They remind us that the Master's presence is inexhaustible, and that every seeker may stumble upon yet another story that touches the heart.

The Unexpected Letter to a Little Boy

A child's simple note of devotion, sent without expectation, received a personal reply from Gurudev himself. The boy's family was astonished, but Gurudev's warmth made clear that sincerity transcends age or status. In the Master's eyes, longing itself is sacred.

The Chopper Landing in the Field

When the skies turned uncertain, Gurudev's helicopter made an emergency landing in Tamil Nadu. Yet devotees recall another moment, quieter and more intimate: while traveling, he asked his driver to stop in a rural field. He walked to a humble farmer's home, where longing had silently burned. The farmer, who could not afford the journey to the ashram, was stunned to see Gurudev at his doorstep.

The Devotee's Daily Food and the Divine Taste

A devotee offered her meals mentally to Gurudev each day, and soon discovered that her food carried a fragrance and taste she could never replicate. Another family recalls Gurudev touching their food, transforming its flavor into something extraordinary. In these moments, the ordinary became divine, infused with the unseen grace of the Master.

The "Child" Who Ate Too Much Pav Bhaji

In Mumbai, teased to eat *dabake*, Gurudev stuffed his mouth in exaggerated delight, dissolving solemnity into laughter. The lesson was clear: spirituality is not divorced from joy; the sacred and the playful coexist.

The Secret of the "Stolen" Item

In candid reflections, Gurudev acknowledged human cravings not as flaws but as conditions to be transcended. This honesty affirms that a Master is not a distant ideal but one who understands and uplifts the human condition.

The "Mistake" That Brought Peace

In a prison program, an inmate told Gurudev, "I am in jail because of you—if you had taught me earlier, I would not have committed these crimes." Gurudev embraced the remark, turning it into a lesson: rehabilitation begins with recognizing the beauty and responsibility within each person.

"I Meet You in Your Heart"

In Delhi, 2014, a devotee feared missing Gurudev due to work. His flight was delayed by exactly two hours, allowing them to meet. When asked for a one-on-one, Gurudev replied: *"Dil mein to milta hoon one to one"*—"In your heart, I always meet you." The words carried a truth beyond time: the Master is never absent, for he dwells in the heart.

The Rs 700 Miracle

In Assam, Gurudev suddenly asked his car to stop, entered a home, and requested a devotee to give Rs 700 to a woman. At that very moment, she was praying for help—her husband's surgery cost Rs 2100, and she was short by exactly Rs 700. Grace had arrived in perfect measure, answering devotion with precision.

The Protective Hand

In Kenya, lions surrounded Gurudev's car, circling it like gentle companions. He sat serene, embodying a deep, unseen connection with nature. What could have been fear became wonder, as creation itself bowed to the presence of peace.

The Transformed Poha

In the early days of the Ashram, Gurudev cooked poha for about 100 people. When a devotee said it tasted "nice," Gurudev chanted over water, poured it into the dish, and asked him to taste again. The flavor had transformed into something heavenly, showing how consciousness itself can infuse matter with divinity.

The Cockpit Struggle

Pilots narrate how, during a flight from Bangalore to Germany, cockpit instruments faltered. Gurudev's calm presence coincided with the GPS resetting and navigation stabilizing. The pilots themselves described it as *"Guru Grace,"* affirming the mysterious ways in which the Master's presence harmonizes even the unseen.

"I Am Responsible"

After a school shooting in the United States, Gurudev said, *"I am responsible—if I would have taught them Sudarshan Kriya and meditation, this would never have happened."* This reflects his profound sense of ownership for humanity's collective consciousness, a conviction that inner peace can transform outer realities.

The Midnight Darshan

Countless devotees recount mystical encounters where Gurudev's presence appeared in dreams, in sudden messages, or in unexpected recognition within crowds. These experiences affirm the Guru tradition: the Master is not confined to a body but is a presence that transcends time and space.

Closing Note

These stories are not the end but a continuation. They remind us that Gurudev's life is a living scripture, unfolding endlessly in letters, laughter, silence, and presence. To read them is to glimpse the infinite—that there is always enough and more to speak of the Master.

And so, the end note becomes not an afterthought, but a prayer:

That the fragrance of his grace may linger,

That the laughter of his play may echo,

That the silence of his presence may abide,

And that the stories of the Master may never cease.

In that quiet recognition, something settles—leaving behind not answers, but a deeper knowing.

Jai Guru Dev!

Victory to the Big Mind.

About The Authors

Prof. Haripriya Rengarajan, a Bengaluru based educationist, author, and researcher, brings over 27 years of expertise spanning the Software, wellness and education sectors. Holding an M.S. in Software Engineering from BITS Pilani, she spearheaded major programs in the software industry before transitioning into a writer, an author and eventually as an educationist.

A distinguished leadership and governance specialist, she serves as visiting faculty at premier universities and B-schools, seamlessly blending corporate acumen with academia. A captivating TEDx speaker, she has addressed global forums on societal transformation through effective leadership, on the power of education, and more. She has also spoken at global leadership forums, including the Agile India Conference.

As a certified yoga teacher, she advocates resilience, balanced leadership, and personal growth, drawing from the depth of ancient wisdom and modern perspectives.

As an eloquent writer, she has authored numerous pieces on leadership, education, wellness, and spirituality. She recently coauthored a book on inner empowerment for women, launched on International Women's Day, amplifying her commitment to fostering strength and self-discovery.

She considers herself a lifelong learner, constantly evolving through her teaching, research, and personal quest for knowledge.

This work on His Holiness, Gurudev Sri Sri Ravishankar is her work of passion in due reverence, gratitude and devotion towards her Master, who brings forth a sense of peace, absolute silence and direction in the journey of life.

Ravi Valluri retired from the Indian Railway Traffic Service as the Principal Chief Commercial Manager, Southern Railway, Chennai and has worked at several places on different zonal railways. He served in Mil Rail (Army Headquarters), where he was decorated with the Chief of Army Staff award.

He also served as CEO of Chhattisgarh East Railway Ltd. & Chhattisgarh East-West Railway Ltd. at Raipur, Chhattisgarh.

Currently he is Advisor, Krishnapatnam Railway Company Limited.

He is the author of several books both (fiction and non-fiction). Besides has contributed to a various anthologies, like *Shattered* curated by Penmancy and a seminal work *India's Long Walk Home* where several prominent authors of India and the world participated. His works have been translated in Telugu, Tamil, Kannada and Hindi.

He is the founder of the literary website www.rustleofwords.com along with his wife Lakshmi Valluri.

He is also a faculty of the Art of Living and conducts the Happiness Programme, yoga and meditation sessions of the Art of Living, besides helping counsel addicts and undertaking courses for that dependant on alcohol and drugs. He has had a penchant for theatre, music public speaking and writing since his school days and continues to fuel these interests. At present, he contributes to The Daily Pioneer, The Daily Guardian Review, Kashmir Times and TelengaTrends.com.

Ravi Valluri has been interviewed by Doordarshan National, Doordarshan Uttar Pradesh and Doordarshan Gorakhpur apart from appearing on Radio FM, Secunderabad and Rainbow FM, Bareilly.

The author can be reached at 9618564024 (WhatsApp) and at valluri.ravi@gmail.com.

https://indpedia.in/wiki/Ravi_Valluri